Hamlet's Mirror

Cover artwork by Zenon Zaporowski from an idea by Tony Butler

Hamlet's Mirror

Shakespeare and the Joy of Theatre

by
Tony Butler

Series *Shakespeare Today* from ShakeUp Press

Published by ShakeUp Press
PO Box 65515
London N3 9BP

www.shakeup.org.uk

ISBN   978-0-9565726-0-8

Printed and bound in Great Britain by
CPI Antony Rowe, Chippenham and Eastbourne

Prove true, imagination, oh prove true.

Twelfth Night   Act III scene iv line 384

Contents

Introduction: Theatre

Our lives are enormously enriched by theatre. It is not just the dramatic enjoyment – we can get much of the same excitement from cinema or television or even a well written novel – but the fact that we are there, alive, thinking and breathing, in the same space where the actors are presenting their alive, pretend characters. The word 'theatre' means both the building and the activity - which Hamlet calls 'playing.' He comments on "the purpose of playing"...

> "... whose end, both at the first and now, was and is, to hold, as 'twere, the mirror up to nature."

It is the purpose of this book to examine some of the ways that Shakespeare constructed that 'mirror' and how we – audience and actors - may more fully understand his intentions.

Shakespeare was, primarily, a poet and writing at a time when theatre as we know it (and 'the theatres') had only been around for twenty years. His experiments and adjustments led to the writing of more than three dozen extraordinary plays unparalleled in world literature – especially in the warm celebration of humanity. It is this aspect along with his joyous manipulation of theatrical effect which is celebrated in the following pages.

Playhouses started to appear in London in 1576 – the first, called The Theatre, was in Shoreditch and was built by James Burbage the father of the actor Richard Burbage, who later took the lead parts in many of Shakespeare's plays. From that moment playwrights flourished. By 1586 Christopher Marlowe had emerged as the most flamboyant, acclaimed for his passion, his spectacle and what Ben Johnson later called "his mighty line" – the pounding rhythms of his verse, which Shakespeare developed into his own instantly recognisable ten syllable line, the rhythms and variations of which became more complex as his writing matured.

Marlowe's mighty verse also helped establish the way actors proclaimed the words on the thrust stages of those new, circular theatre buildings where audiences went "to hear a play".

Added to this was the excitement of the rediscovery of ancient literature. The plays of ancient Greece – Aeschylus, Euripides, Aristophanes – were only known via Latin translations, but the Roman plays of Terence and Plautus, after a gap of more than a thousand years, were now known and performed. Theatre was, therefore, a true 'renaissance' activity, not new but reborn, and growing to extraordinary maturity: captivating, provocative, highly enjoyable and – like music, painting, sculpture, and dance – awakening human interest in realms beyond the everyday.

By 1596 the new activity of Theatre had been around for twenty years. It is probable that discussion of the validity of 'acting', the absurdity of 'performance', and the incompetence of actors, amateur and professional, was, at this time, a very modern topic - and Shakespeare could hardly resist taking part. So in the remarkable *Midsummer Night's Dream* - one of the half dozen plays in which there is a play within the play – he gives us Duke Theseus's thoughts on acting and theatre.

About the same time he wrote *Romeo and Juliet* and *Richard II.* These three plays are a peak of perfection: they blend poetry and drama into seamless compositions, works of art that shine for all time. What he has perfected is Poetic Drama.

If Shakespeare had died in 1596 - and his plays written by then had survived - we would have material enough to say he was a great poet and dramatic craftsman. But fortunately he lived: and, miraculously, his unsatisfied genius went on enquiring and experimenting. He was encouraged by the building of the Globe Theatre in 1599 and the prominence of his company, The Lord Chamberlain's Men, who periodically performed for Queen Elizabeth. On the accession of the new king, James I in 1603, this company of players became The King's Men, thereby acquiring great prestige. Plays were the property of the companies that performed them. They were not often printed or published. Praise then for Ben Jonson, a fellow playwright, and the surviving actors of the company who put together 37 of Shakespeare's plays and published them in 1623 – seven years after his death, twelve years after his last great play, *The Tempest*. It is this collection of printed scripts, generally referred to as the First Folio, which gives us his complete works. Without it he would hardly be known.

The three great tragedies *Othello, Macbeth,* and *King Lear* were probably written in the years 1604–06. Before that, 1599-1600, is *Hamlet* - a play which provokes intense questions and endless discussion. It also seems to contain many personal connections – to Shakespeare, to any actor who performs the lead role, and to individual listeners and readers.

Hamlet's enthusiasm when he meets the actors who have come to visit Elsinore lifts him out of his present melancholy. He himself speaks a speech which he then hands over to the First Player; he commissions the troupe to act a play for the court; and he gives advice on how they should perform - along with the comments on the purpose of playing.

The full text of Hamlet's advice to the actors - as it appears in the First Folio - is printed on pages 88 - 89. In the chapters which precede this a number of aspects and ingredients of Shakespeare's plays are considered:

First: the fantasy worlds in which the plays are set.

Second: the characters - their creation, and the way that Shakespeare's love of life and amazement at human possibility imbues them with such attractive vitality, and creates such joy - portraits of soldiers, lovers, tyrants and tapsters that fill the worlds of our imagination.

Third: the importance of that 'Imagination' – the actors', the playwright's and the audience's. This is Chapter 5.

And Fourth, in Chapter 6, consideration of the primary ingredient of drama: Passion. In his instructions to the actors it is the portrayal of this Passion that Hamlet particularly cares about:

> *...it offends me to the Soul, to see a robustious Pery-wig-pated Fellow, tear a Passion to tatters, to very rags, to split the ears of the Groundlings: who (for the most part) are capable of nothing, but inexplicable dumb shows, ...*

... but within moments he says: *Be not too tame neither.*

How do you get the balance? Shakespeare's concern – and Hamlet's - is that the players (the actors) may be heard and appreciated by the audience. The mingling of Hamlet with Shakespeare himself, make this speech especially interesting.

In exploring this – and other pieces of text throughout the book – the technique is to pursue *the words*: their apparent meanings, their hidden meanings, their sounds and associations. It is the effect of his words on us, today, that determines our response. Historical, scholarly information might colour our perception (if we know about it) but is of little use to most theatre-goers as they listen to the play.

The Mirror which is – "as it were" – held up to Nature shows a number of things:

> *Virtue her own Feature, Scorn her own Image, and the very Age and Body of the Time, his form and pressure.*

This seems to suggest that more than character and situation is presented in theatre. And it is the very extraordinary way in which the audience – as well as the actors – take part in any performance which makes the investigation of Shakespeare's intentions so fascinating.

1: Miranda's Surprise.

How beauteous mankind is! O brave new world,
That has such people in it!

The Tempest V i 184 – 185

Taking our seat in a theatre, even before the action begins, we commit ourselves to entering the world inhabited by the people of the play. Here, now, we are captive in this space – with them. And in this space they create a world for themselves and for us.

All Shakespeare's characters speak directly to us. Whatever they say to each other is also said to each member of the audience. So we are involved, not just in imagination - through empathy and emotional identity (which can also be experienced in the novel) – but in reality: here is an actual person speaking in this space where we are present. Sometimes the actor is alone on stage and we are the only people to whom the words are spoken: such is the manner of this speaking that, when she chooses, an actor may address remarks to individual members of the audience, or to a selected group, as Rosalind does in her epilogue to *As You Like It* when she 'conjures' first the women – "I charge you, Oh women, for the love you bear to men..." - and then the men. But the same personal, direct, impact upon each of us may be experienced when logically the speaker is talking to another 'character'.

Let us follow up this idea in *The Tempest*. This is the last of Shakespeare's great plays: being such - he knew he would not write another - we might expect him to draw upon and draw together many of the interesting and exciting things he had learnt to put into a play. We are not disappointed.

The opening scene: a ship - a storm at sea. This is 'the tempest' which is about to spill a large number of 'characters' who are struggling and shouting on the deck of the ship into the sea and onto the island. Prospero's island. Shakespeare's island. The island which is the play.

A few minutes into the second scene Prospero, the master magician of the play, asks his daughter, Miranda, whether she can remember ..

A time before we came unto this cell?

The Tempest I ii 39

And the question immediately confronts us with the magic of theatre. Suppose the play stopped at this moment and that some of the thoughts which – while the play is playing – remain in the back our minds, were to be heard. What are *we* doing here? What is the connection between us and Miranda? What is the relative existence and reality of the here and now compared with the "time before *we* came unto this....." theatre, play, island – "cell"? We are recent arrivals: we have been here about twenty minutes. Miranda has been here most of her life.

- - - - -

Aside. The "cell" is the cave in which Prospero and his daughter live – on the island. It is interesting that he uses this word. Almost the only other use of the word in Shakespeare is for Friar Laurence's cell in ***Romeo and Juliet***. [There is also a Friar Patrick whose cell is referred to and used as a meeting place in ***Two Gentlemen of Verona***. Patrick himself never appears.] So the word carries with it an image of the monkish, shut away, unadorned yet secret, clever, holy place. Friar Laurence, it will be recalled, mixes his herbal drugs here: from his cupboard he takes the frightening brew that puts Juliet into a death-like trance. It is already prepared: it sits on the shelf alongside – we must suppose – many other medicines (and poisons?). And Prospero keeps his magic books in his 'cell'. With the help of these he has raised the storm. And instead of saying 'island' - or simply 'place' - it is "this cell" in the question put to his daughter – and to us. Are we, the listeners to the play, in "a cell"? How separate is that from the world 'before'? And can we escape the other meaning of the word that

14

may be sounding in our (and Miranda's) head: the prison cell? For if we truly have been *imprisoned* by Prospero – or Shakespeare - on this island, with faded memories of the world outside, what does Life hold stored for us?

- - - - -

How much *does* she remember?　More than her father suspects.

> PROSPERO.　　　*Canst thou remember*
> *A time before we came unto this cell?*
> *I do not think thou canst; for then thou wast not*
> *Out three years old.*
> MIRANDA.　　　　*Certainly, sir, I can.*
> PROSPERO. *By what? By any other house, or person?*
> *Of any thing the image, tell me, that*
> *Hath kept with thy remembrance?*
> MIRANDA.　　　　　　　*'Tis far off,*
> *And rather like a dream than an assurance*
> *That my remembrance warrants. Had I not*
> *Four, or five, women once, that tended me?*
> PROSPERO. *Thou hadst, and more, Miranda.*
> *But how is it*
> *That this lives in thy mind? What seest thou else*
> *In the dark backward and abysm of time?*

The Tempest I ii 38 -50

So the strange, disturbing image of "the dark backward and abysm of time" – momentarily surfacing in Prospero's mind - passes without comment.

But suppose all action were to stop at *this* moment and we were allowed more than the briefest interval of time to linger over this abyss – glancing back to the unknown origins of time and history, to ponder the mythical darkness – the actual darkness – from which consciousness, life itself, emerged so long ago. The trivial particulars of our own brief lives, waiting for us when we

15

return to daylight and reasonableness after the show, do – *must* – somehow, relate to the deep, dark origins of all things. And theatre is here to remind us now and then of such extraordinary, inexplicable things. In this case: how we came here. But Prospero is in the middle of a long, important piece of family explanation, and the necessary action of plot and story, leaves us no time for contemplation.

It is twelve years since Prospero and his baby daughter were expelled from Milan, put into a leaky boat and left to the mercy of wind and waves: a sea voyage not unlike that of another child and parent in ancient Greek legend, Perseus and his mother Danae. It *is* a mythological or dream event – as all the past is "rather like a dream" to Miranda.

Growing up on the island she had only her father and the strange creature who is condemned - indeed *defined* by her father - as a wicked monster. When he first came to the island, Prospero was kind to Caliban....

> ... *and lodg'd thee*
> *In mine own cell, till thou didst seek to violate*
> *The honour of my child.*

> *CALIBAN. O ho, O ho! Would't had been done.*
> *Thou didst prevent me; I had peopl'd else*
> *This isle with Calibans.*

The Tempest I ii 348 - 353

So alongside the humanist education given to her by her father she is not ignorant of sex and danger.

Now on the threshold of womanhood Miranda has been alerted to the intrusion of the outside world by seeing the shipwreck. Reality has arrived. Any moment now she will be setting eyes on a young man from the wrecked ship who believes himself to be the only survivor of the terrible tempest. And she will fall instantly in love.

He, whose name is Ferdinand, is, of course, a Prince.

16

What absurd fairy-tale is this? Did we come to the theatre to be confronted by such absurdity, folk-lore, myth, romance, fantasy? How, among the worries and practicalities of our lives, should we be spending time (and money) visiting such islands – or cells? Is this what Art is about?

Maybe. There is, for example, a possibly illuminating parallel between Miranda's experience and the 'normal' experience which any pubescent girl grows through. Cosseted on the real island of her own imagination a child creates the world. Gradually or suddenly external 'realities' of unpredictable adults, natural and man-made violence, bodily awareness and sex, come to adjust that world. To be given a fantastical poetic picture of the process is to confirm rather than contradict the naturalness and necessity of the adjustment. Miranda's quick awakening is a symbolic telling.

So theatre offers us a poetic interpretation of some aspects of life. Can it also offer a blunt confrontation: clarity rather than poetry? Miranda's father speaks of his role:

Here in this island .... here
Have I, thy schoolmaster, made thee more profit
Than other princesses can, that have more time
For vainer hours, and tutors not so careful.

The Tempest I ii 171 - 4

This play is Shakespeare's last major work. The epilogue with which it ends is sometimes identified as Shakespeare's farewell to the theatre. Of all his plays it is the most fantastical – even more so than **Midsummer Night's Dream**. And yet Shakespeare, *our* schoolmaster, also has some serious, down-to-earth telling to do in this play.

On the one hand an image from a song give us the picture. Prince Ferdinand, wandering the island alone, believes that his father, the king of Naples, has drowned. Out of the air comes to him a "ditty" that "does remember my drowned father" which contains the lines:

17

Nothing of him doth fade,
But doth suffer a sea-change
Into something rich and strange.

The Tempest I ii 403 - 405

And this might be taken as a comment on Shakespeare's final play: nothing of the master playwright-poet "doth fade" but here is indeed a sea-change:

Into something rich and strange.

On the other hand our "careful tutor" offers us a banquet in which Caliban, the exotic monster, and Ariel, the fiery spirit, play scenes with Trinculo, the jester, and Stephano, the King's butler. Grief, guilt, love, laughter, anger, horror, innocence and villainy shout and chatter their ways through this play. A masque is staged by spirits, who, earlier have presented – yes - a banquet to the King and the wicked brothers (it is, of course, only an illusion. The food vanishes and Ariel appears in the guise of a 'harpy' – a most terrifying, vengeful mythical creature). This King, early in the play, laments the marriage of his daughter, lost to an alien culture for the sake of political alliance – and finally, at the end of the play, approves the marriage of his son to make a political alliance with Duke Prospero whom he has previously attempted to destroy. So much, and so much more: a pageant of the practical and political weaving its way through a magical world of imagination. Practical considerations made palatable by fantasy.

- - - - -

Aside: the King's daughter's name is Claribel. Where does Shakespeare get his names from? No doubt there is some well informed answer to that, but, for those whose minds look for conspiracy and poetry, is it not strange that the names Claribel and Caliban share the same emphasis and number of syllables and several letters?

- - - - -

18

From this play comes, famously, this definition of life:

> *We are such stuff*
> *As dreams are made on; and our little life*
> *Is rounded with a sleep.*

The Tempest IV i 156 - 158

Prospero has just staged - and then interrupted - a masque performed by spirits. As it vanishes he remarks that it was an "insubstantial pageant" and a "baseless fabric" – that is something of no real 'substance', a 'fabrication' with no actual roots - or 'base'. The performance was 'real' enough: the spectators saw it, heard it, understood the plot and lyrics – but it was all in imagination. It was Theatre.

- - - - -

Aside. It is worth remarking that this brief quotation is often misquoted – and spoken as if the line was:

> *We are such stuff as dreams are made of...*

- "of" replacing "on". As such it makes sense and surprises - is thought-provoking: "*We* are 'made' of the same stuff **as** dreams"? But that is not quite what he writes.

- - - - -

Of all playwrights Shakespeare is among those most conscious of the 'theatre' aspects of our thoughts and actions. And of the importance of fantasy, story, dream and the 'theatrical' if we are ever to make any sense of our lives.

More than that. If we are to consider ourselves as being the "stuff" that "dreams are made *on*" we need to clarify the image, to spot the identify of this "stuff" on which the dreams are "made". The clearest answer is that it is the cloth on which a tapestry might be woven ('cloth' is still one of the meanings of 'stuff' in the modern Chambers Dictionary). If this is so it implies that dreams and imagination are more real, or at least more significant, than

19

'the material' on which they are implanted. The substance of our bodies – brains and all - is as nothing compared to the 'reality' of the imagination.

- - - - -

Aside. In remembering the quote we are tempted to write:

> *We are such stuff as dreams are made on,*
> *And our little life is rounded with a sleep.*

Or, if we are looking for the regular ten beat line:

> *We are such stuff as dreams are made on - and*
> *Our little life is rounded with a sleep.*

Both these are fine: perhaps the second (if you try speaking it aloud) gives the thought process a more substantial airing. But – although in *hearing* the text (or indeed in *speaking* it) there is nothing to prevent either of those word patterns predominating - the actual appearance in the printed text is as given on the previous page. Throughout this play the verse contains many rhythmical units which begin in the middle of a line and end in the middle of the next line. And many lines 'break the rules' by having an extra (or a missing) syllable. Well spoken this presents no problem to the ear: driven, colourful, urgent, tuneful – all the verse (and prose) of this play is captivating. But *speaking* it well is less easy: the density and complexity demands awareness, skill and hard work.

- - - - -

Let us return to Miranda whose awakening to life is one of the plays main concerns. She half remembers women around her when she was a baby but, as she says when she meets Prince Ferdinand, of men she has only known her father and the monster Caliban:

20

> *This*
> *Is the third man that e'er I saw – the first*
> *That e'er I sighed for.*
>
> **The Tempest** I ii **450**

Her falling in love with him at first sight – a meeting engineered by Ariel, Prospero's servant/slave - delights her father:

> *At first sight*
> *They have changed eyes. Delicate Ariel,*
> *I'll set thee free for this.*
>
> **The Tempest** I ii **446**

But he is careful to *seem* opposed to the union of his daughter and this prince. First, he accuses Ferdinand of being a spy and a traitor; then he disarms him; and finally he turns on his daughter:

> *Silence: one word more*
> *Shall make me chide thee, if not hate thee: what?*
> *An advocate for an impostor! Hush*
> *Thou think'st there is no more such shapes as he,*
> *Having seen but him and Caliban…*
>
> **The Tempest** I ii **483**

Is this a 'pretence' at anger? Or is Prospero not quite in control of his emotions? He is possessed by a fury which has grown over the years and bursts out against Caliban and – surprisingly, earlier in this scene - against Ariel (who is bargaining for his freedom and complained "is there more toil?" [I ii 242]). Now Prospero's feelings about Miranda also seem tainted by this fury, which is quite a surprise for her: later she says, "Never till this day, saw I him touched with anger," [IV i 145]. The relationship between fathers and daughters is much explored by Shakespeare; not least in this play and at this moment. The complexities of motive and emotion are many: the more we ponder the script the more questions emerge.

Within the span of its 500 lines this scene moves from the witness of the shipwreck, through the history of father and daughter, to the meetings with monster and spirit (and hearing *their* histories), to seeing the Prince, entranced by Ariel's song,

21

weep for his father - and fall in love. Written by anyone else this would be a whole play! It's ending sets the dilemma for any young lovers: the need to be together and the harsh conditions that fate and parents impose to hinder this. Shakespeare constructs the scenario: Prospero manipulates the conditions.

- - - - -

Aside. Some commentators see the whole play as Prospero's fantasy - and there are theatre productions where he is presented as the director or *the dreamer* of the play.

- - - - -

From the moment of meeting Ferdinand, Miranda's journey through the play is entirely bound up with her love for him. That is until the miraculous moment when, disturbed in a cave playing with him (at chess!), she is suddenly presented with the sight – the presence – of "many goodly creatures".

The people she sees are King Alonso of Naples, his wicked brother Sebastian, the courtiers, and her own wicked uncle, Prospero's brother Antonio. *We* know the three royals were guilty of banishing Prospero from Milan, his dukedom - and the near death of him and Miranda thirteen years ago. In the course of the play *we* have watched Antonio and Sebastian plot to murder Alonso.

But for Miranda:

O, wonder!
How many goodly creatures are there here!
How beauteous mankind is! O brave new world,
That has such people in it!

The Tempest V i 181 - 184

Prospero responds with a half line that often gets a laugh in the theatre:

'Tis new to thee.

22

Prospero knows what we know. Not only does this group of people contain the "three men of sin" [III iii 53] but it is representative of an old and far from brave world of power-seeking self-seeking people. Prospero's – and our – cynical chuckle at Miranda's innocence is appropriate. Realistic. But sad. As the play ends she is about to be launched into the 'real' world of Naples and Milan. As a future Queen, how will she fare?

And we, nearing the end of our short spell on the island of this play, are about to leave the theatre and return to our 'real' world. How will we fare? Can we take Miranda's words as an appropriate exclamation, when we next observe the "goodly creatures" around us? Probably not! But as an appropriate observation of the creatures who inhabit Shakespeare's plays they will do well enough. We are drawn into a world ...

That has such people in it!

The Tempest is printed as the first play in the Folio of 1623 and this order is still maintained in copies of The Collected Works.

Is there some comment here? Are we to take it that the original editors deliberately shipwrecked us into the whole collection by putting *this* first scene first, with the thought that *this* play demands a fanciful, creative perusal *which then applies to all the plays.* History, also, is dream. Comedy, tragedy, laughter, pain – *all* is part of our little life rounded, bounded, filled out and enlarged by dream and sleep and theatre.

To be able to leave our everyday world and enter the world created by the actors is a wonderful experience. Modern invention has extended the possibilities of such adventure: there are virtual worlds where we can invent new lives for ourselves on the internet; powerful evocations of space among the planets, and journeys deep into the ocean in new cinema – technologies which have been developing since the revolutionary arrival early in the twentieth century of Radio and recorded sound.

Listening demands the concentration which poetry requires. Listening to a Shakespeare play on radio [or tape/CD etc.] is one way to ensure that we really pay attention to the words – the poetry. Even the simplest of lines contains images which conjure associations in our minds.

- - - - -

Aside. So, for example, in a line quoted above [page 21] Prospero accuses Miranda of being "An advocate for an impostor". Two Latin words which connect to the legal role of an 'advocate', alien words from a father to a daughter, pushing the encounter into the world of politics and law when it was, for her, a vision of love. Notice how the rattling consonants of these words, requiring considerable contortions of lips and mouth if spoken strongly (as they obviously are), add to the severity. Hearing these words both Miranda and we are forced to link up to political reality: in her case, if he and she are princes, what implications for Naples and Milan? In our case: is this play as much about state matters and international conflict as any of the History plays? The brief but proper 'hearing' of the words conjures some such associations: the picture in our mind passes in a flash – but there it is.

- - - - -

Watching a play, the antics of the actors – or of the audience - may be a distraction. If we could manage to keep up the 'listening' attentiveness of a radio performance while adding the visual and collective all-of-us-here-together aspects so vital to 'live theatre' – why then we would have the full, true experience that theatre promises. And, probably, most theatre-goers have had such moments, or if they have been very lucky, whole performances when it really 'worked': the shared experience, the compelled imprisonment in the enclosed space, and the complete, attentive 'hearing' of the play.

These ingredients are especially needed when we are present at a Shakespeare play. Many other pieces of drama are just as good on television or in a cinema as on stage – but not Shakespeare.

Firstly, the script is written to be spoken *at* the audience: this is the way it was written – Shakespeare building on Marlowe's technique, which in its turn was the child of the new theatre spaces invented in England at this time.

Secondly, the poetic content – the style of word collection in each line – demands an imaginative response (sometimes conscious; often unconscious) whereby the conjured images fall out of the mouth of the actor into our minds. These images are both single (a concrete picture/item created by a single word: e.g. "cell" in the discussion above) and collective (phrases such as "stuff that dreams are made on") and the mingled crowd of them pours into our ears, and with luck into our brains, where the imagination stores material for dream and prophecy and life.

2: Richard's Prison.

Thus play I in one person many people.

Richard II   V   v   31

Shakespeare the creator of "such people".

In 400 years how many times have these many people been heard, each one stepping into view - on stage, always different, always new created by the actor's skill.

Or living in the mind of the attentive reader.

What people these are! Hamlet, Hotspur, Helen of Troy (in *Troilus and Cressida*); Cleopatra, Rosalind, Phoebe and Audrey (in *As You Like It*); princes, murderers, prostitutes, earls, tapsters, seafaring men and crowds of energetic, adventurous, young men and women from Verona, Warwickshire, ancient Rome, ancient Britain, Vienna (in *Measure for Measure*), Scotland, France, Sicily, Bohemia, Illyria....

Ghosts. Spirits. Caliban, and the three weird sisters....

And all those Kings: Lear, two Richards (II and III – what a contrast!), three Henrys (in six plays), John, Duncan, Macbeth, Cymbeline, Alonso (of Naples) and Ferdinand (of Navarre in *Loves Labours Lost*). And Claudius King of Dennmark.

Julius Caesar; Viola; Malvolio; Desdemona; Sir Andrew Aguecheek.

The list goes on and on. Every one of them – even if speaking merely seven or eight lines – may be thought through, fleshed out, admired, sympathised with, cared about, accused....... identified as failing and succeeding in the game of life. Just as we watch our neighbours and our children, or despair of our parents or public figures, just so can we ponder the behaviour of each of these people, as real as people we have met or seen – more real sometimes!

What sort of mind was capable of such bringing-to-life?

As it happens Shakespeare has written a scene in which someone sets out to do exactly that. *Richard II* ends with the king, alone in prison, desperately humiliated, attempting to populate his world. It is a fruitless exercise but full of interesting observations and the very fact that he sets out on this task, not unlike that of the playwright before the first word is written, is worth our attention.

Part of the effectiveness of this scene, this play, and all Shakespeare's plays which have Kings and Queens as their main protagonists, is in the identification of the 'ordinary' observer with this royal person, who is, anyway, only another human being. This king, Richard II, was deposed by Henry Bolingbroke who became King Henry IV and the play recalls the irresponsible, sad, sensitive life of Richard, and the justification for Bolingbroke's ambitious action. As a piece of English history worthy of dramatisation it is a politically sensitive subject – putting on a performance of this play and thereby publicly performing the removal of a monarch from the throne was a provocative act, especially during the last years of Queen Elizabeth's reign

Richard was an unjust, irresponsible king. We may agree with those who would un-king him that he *is* vain and vacillating, but having followed him through the play we feel for him. Now, out of his loneliness, comes this extraordinary mixture of images and philosophies. Richard's prison is like Prospero's (or Friar Laurence's) cell: full of clever things - in this case not in books or bottles but in the mind.

Listening to this speech [Richard II V v 1-41] we hardly have time to digest it all. It is worth, therefore, examining it bit by bit. In doing so we will note how our thoughts are directed inward and outward: deeper into the character and the situation of the scene, and out towards our own understanding of the world. This, in turn, throws light on something of the process that Shakespeare employs, here and throughout his plays.

The speech is crammed with contradictions - which turns it into an independent drama on its own. As our attention follows Richard's leaping thoughts, so we partake of the drama – even, perhaps, *feeling* the emotional twists and opposites that he leads us through. Identification with the speaker (empathy = the power of imaginatively experiencing another's experience) is demanded by six uses of " I " in the first six lines and another eight in ten lines at the end.

- - - - -

Aside. Unless, of course, this causes us to reject him for his self–centeredness. Advice to an actor playing Richard: beware too much self pity.

- - - - -

Here then is the speech, broken up into sections which generally mark a shift of thought, but are primarily there to help digest the rich feast of Richard's imagination.

KING RICHARD. *I have been studying how I may compare*
This prison where I live unto the world.
And, for because the world is populous
And here is not a creature but myself,
I cannot do it.
                         Yet I'll hammer it out.
My brain I'll prove the female to my soul,
My soul the father......
                    ... and these two beget
A generation of still-breeding thoughts,
And these same thoughts people this little world,
In humours like the people of this world,
For no thought is contented.
                         The better sort,
As thoughts of things divine, are intermix'd
With scruples, and do set the Faith itself

28

Against the Faith,   As thus:
'Come, little ones'; and then again,
'It is as hard to come as for a camel
To thread the postern of a small needle's eye.'
Thoughts tending to ambition, they do plot
Unlikely wonders: how these vain weak nails
May tear a passage through the flinty ribs
Of this hard world, my ragged prison walls;
And, for they cannot, die in their own pride.

Thoughts tending to content flatter themselves
That they are not the first of fortune's slaves,
Nor shall not be the last; like silly beggars
Who, sitting in the stocks, refuge their shame,
That many have and others must sit there;
And in this thought they find a kind of ease,
Bearing their own misfortunes on the back
Of such as have before endur'd the like.

Thus play I in one person many people,
And none contented.

Sometimes am I king;
Then treasons make me wish myself a beggar,
And so I am.
                    Then crushing penury
Persuades me I was better when a king;
Then am I king'd again;
                        and by and by
Think that I am unking'd by Bolingbroke,
And straight am nothing.

But whate'er I be,
Nor I, nor any man that but man is,
With nothing shall be pleas'd till he be eas'd
With being nothing.

Richard II   V v 1 – 41

Let us take this speech now, section by section. Having first
noted that dividing it up in this way most segments begin (and/or

29

end) in the middle of a line – the flow of King Richard's thought hesitates and moves not quite directly forward at each of these points. Two exceptions to this are the segments where his pondering of the action or objective thought (tearing at the prison walls; accepting "they are not the first") is more controlled than his self-reflective thinking. These two sections are also the most flowing (*and* easiest to comprehend) making a rolling-on, tuneful centre of *the music* of the whole piece. Later this becomes a series of compressed cries, each with a switch-back emotional journey : e.g. penury [pain] – thought [hope] – king'd again [triumph]. This musicality is, of course, fundamental to the whole of Shakespeare's writing: rhythm, pace, variety of emphasis and grammatical complexity, combine to make both the speaking and the 'hearing' of the text an artistic pursuit. Audiences as well as actors need practice!

The world that Richard wishes to fill with people is the world of his prison – where there is no-one but himself.

> *KING RICHARD. I have been studying how I may compare*
> *This prison where I live unto the world.*
> *And, for because the world is populous*
> *And here is not a creature but myself,*
> *I cannot do it.*

Dejection. Loss of action. Dramatic decision: action -

> *Yet I'll hammer it out.*

And we note the resource to a "hammer" – a real, hard, practical tool brought into the realm of thought. Not the first time this hammer has been called up by Shakespeare: in one of his first plays, *Titus Andronicus*, the villain Aaron tells us that "Blood and revenge are hammering in my head" [II iii 49]. If only it were a real hammer that might help him escape his prison – but he has only his "vain weak nails" to attack the walls (though we might note "hammer" and "nails" make a matching pair!)

Richard wants to 'populate' his prison:

My brain I'll prove the female to my soul,
My soul the father......

The brain and the soul. Mother, father – female, male.
Which is which? If we attach gender to them, we might think the
brain more male - logical, controlling; and the soul more womanly.
Certainly Hamlet refers to the soul as feminine. In his speech to
his friend Horatio he says:

> *Since my dear soul was mistress of her choice,*
> *And could of men distinguish - her election*
> *Hath sealed thee for herself.*

Hamlet III ii 62 –65

It is hard to decide whether there is an issue here. Given the
inevitable debate as to what exactly we mean by 'soul', and
allowing that Richard [or Shakespeare] may have plunged into this
metaphorical allocation of gender without much thought, there is
nevertheless a temptation to speculate. Is there some inner
confusion of sexual identity in Richard? The play touches on his
bi-sexual nature: one of the accusations against him was that he
paid more attention to the young men about court than he did to
his wife.

As it is, brain and soul:

> *... these two beget*
> *A generation of still-breeding thoughts,*
> *And these same thoughts people this little world,*
> *In humours like the people of this world,*
> *For no thought is contented.*

He sees "the people of this world" (that is the 'real' world) as
discontented: to match them, "no thought is contented".   We
might question whether this is valid comment or a reflection of his
own sad state.

The word "still-breeding" supposedly means that these
thoughts are 'still' (continually) going on 'breeding' (reproducing

themselves), but lurking within this phrase is the word 'still-born' (dead) and the suggestion that Richard's exercise is futile.

But he keeps working at it.

> *The better sort,*
> *As thoughts of things divine, are intermix'd*
> *With scruples, and do set the Faith itself*
> *Against the Faith,   As thus:*
> *'Come, little ones'; and then again,*
> *'It is as hard to come as for a camel*
> *To thread the postern of a small needle's eye.'*

These direct quotations from the New Testament are contradictory, setting "the Faith itself against the Faith". The first [St Luke - chapter 18 verse 16] refers to Jesus welcoming little children to the kingdom of heaven, while the second [St Matthew 19 v 24] reminds us how hard it is for a rich man to get into that kingdom. Richard seems to be saying that however much religion gives us the "better" thoughts, we will still meet contradictions.

- - - - -

Aside.   Biblical quotations (and mis-quotations) occur frequently throughout Shakespeare. It is rare that they come with such deliberate exactness.

- - - - -

He now begins to list and analyse the discontent of his people/thoughts:

> *Thoughts tending to ambition, they do plot*
> *Unlikely wonders: how these vain weak nails*
> *May tear a passage through the flinty ribs*
> *Of this hard world, my ragged prison walls;*
> *And, for they cannot, die in their own pride.*

Should "ragged" read "rugged" – or has the 'ragged' state of the prisoner become attached to the prison?   As the final phrase runs its course, we might speculate (if we had time) how it will end. "Die in their own...." – what do we expect? Despair? Futility? But what is provided is a word that lifts our spirits in the final moment of these down-beat lines. It does so both with meaning *and* with sound, picking up the bright pronunciation of "likely", "flinty", "rib", "pris..", "die" to end with "pride". The very verse is itself an "unlikely wonder"! The images, characteristically, include parts of the body: nails and ribs. But the 'flinty' ribs are the prison bars, and the prison walls make the 'hard world' "through" which his ambition wishes to "tear a passage".

- - - - -

Aside. Does that phrase have a navigational tang to it? The ship of life hopefully finding a 'passage' through the seas of the world – but in this case having to "tear" a passage: like the warrior Macbeth who "carved out his passage" through the rebel army to face the 'merciless Macdonwald' [Macbeth I ii 19]. Amusingly Hamlet's disdain of the loud-mouthed actor whom he hears *"tear a passion* to tatters" [Hamlet III ii 9] lurks here. Shakespeare's mind leaps wildly among the metaphors of court, seamanship, the human body, law, hunting, money.... To recognise each of these is to be enriched: *our* minds snatching up images from every corner of life.

- - - - -

Thoughts tending to content, flatter themselves
That they are not the first of fortune's slaves,
Nor shall not be the last; like silly beggars
Who, sitting in the stocks, refuge their shame,
That many have and others must sit there;
And in this thought they find a kind of ease,
Bearing their own misfortunes on the back
Of such as have before endur'd the like.

33

Here, with a philosophical view of hardship, is the most logical, coherent section of the whole speech. Eight lines: one sentence. A beautifully composed piece including the marvellous phrase "refuge their shame".

As he proceeds, 'the world' ceases to be the prison, and becomes his own mind – or body. And when he comes to the line "thus play I in one person many people" he ceases to be just the playwright: he becomes also an actor.

> *Thus play I in one person many people,*
> *And none contented.*

But that meaning shifts again when I discover that in some texts, including the Folio, "person" has become "prison":

> *Thus play I in one prison many people.*

- - - - -

Aside. Scholarly editing of Shakespeare's texts has been a major intellectual activity since the eighteenth century. The extracts in this book are based on the Folio - sometimes with altered punctuation. This is the least offensive change that an editor can make, and there are many actors who would reserve the right to alter the punctuation yet again if they feel that a stronger (or different) meaning can thereby be achieved. The justification for changing a *word* (especially if this can be done by the simple change of one or two letters) may be based on a claim that the type-setter of the original printing got it wrong, or that the actual manuscript offered the typesetter was, anyway, for some reason corrupt (or unreadable). Whole libraries could be filled with the queries and theories expounded in the search for Shakespeare's "true original' wording.

- - - - -

Now Richard comes to the point. Is he a king or not?

34

> *Sometimes am I king;*
> *Then treasons make me wish myself a beggar,*
> *And so I am.*

Who acts these "treasons"? Since all is in his mind, is it him acting against himself?

> *Then crushing penury*
> *Persuades me I was better when a king;*
> *Then am I king'd again;*
> > *and by and by*
> *Think that I am unking'd by Bolingbroke,*
> *And straight am nothing.*

Truth. Henry Bolingbroke it is who having driven Richard from the throne – "unking'd" him – rules as King Henry IV.

And now his conclusion, drawing upon the powerful concept of "nothing".

> *But whate'er I be,*
> *Nor I, nor any man that but man is,*
> *With nothing shall be pleas'd till he be eas'd*
> *With being nothing.*

This "any man that but man is" links *us* – and everyone - to Richard: the word "eas'd" (ending the last but one line) linking back to the men in the stocks, who knowing that they share their shame with so many others, thereby "find a kind of ease".

Such little steps as these are the weapons of poetry. Twisting our recognition to reconsider the whole at every moment.

At the point where we have ended this speech there is an interruption: music plays - and the subject of his thought shifts to incorporate harmony/discord and time (keeping time, time passing, wasting time...).

The word "nothing" three times at the end (each with a slight shift in use and meaning) leads us back to the empty prison cell of the first section where there is "not a creature" – no thing.

35

Is this prison also the human body in which the soul is trapped – till it be "eased" out into eternity? Or oblivion? Nothing. Nothing. Nothing. We have to be careful here. This word reappears too often in the works of Shakespeare for us to let it pass without question. The title he chooses for one of his plays might apply to them all: *Much Ado about Nothing.* And King Lear is mistaken when he says,

> *Nothing will come of nothing.*
>
> King Lear I i 89

... since the whole of the hopeful part of the plot of that play grows out of his daughter Cordelia's silence: it is she who, asked what she has to say that will prove her love for her father, replies "Nothing".

So: does this description by Richard of his attempt to populate his prison world give us any glimpse into Shakespeare's creation of character? Certainly Richard tries to describe the process of imagining - but does he really create people?

And what about those interesting male and female elements which 'beget' the thoughts? In Richard's scheme, the 'brain' (intellect) being the female (who supposedly 'gives birth' and 'creates' the specific detail of each person/thought) and the 'soul' identified as male (who impregnates the intellect?). This, as already mentioned above, is the reverse of the gender association normally attached to brain and soul in Shakespeare and in Western European culture: the rational, ordering intellect generally being identified with the male, while the mysterious intuitive functions of feeling and soul are seen as female.

Maybe this is no more than saying that *both* imagination and intellect (female and male attributes?) feed the creative process. But attempts at creation are not necessarily successful. Richard's thought-people have no characteristics: they tear at the walls, they sit in the stocks, they think treason, and they despair of deserving royal status, but they have no 'visible' attributes. Maybe this is because Richard is completely taken up with his own

36

emotional and physical disaster: all his 'thoughts' are self attentive. We may question, therefore, whether he really does "play ... many people". He dabbles in many emotional varieties of self assurance – and fails to find any. He fails to find any person other than himself.

Whereas Shakespeare....! One of the enduring frustrations that has haunted readers and critics over the centuries is that we cannot find the man, the 'real' emotional Shakespeare in his characters. He is never bound up in *his own* feelings. It is the people he creates who have lively functional specific attributes and feelings which are their own. They come to life as individuals. They are not Shakespeare.

Richard, then, is a character in a Shakespeare play who, like so many others, reveals himself to us. And it is Shakespeare's craftsmanship that fleshes him out. But he, in turn, does not posses Shakespeare's skill in creating other people. His "thoughts" remain inside his head. The only script he gives his 'people' to speak are quotes from the New Testament. No living, speaking-in-their-own-voices, characters here.

The interesting people whom Shakespeare creates, think for themselves. Among the stars are many of his heroines: Juliet, Rosalind, Miranda and Marina (in **Pericles**), Beatrice... with all of whom an inner passion over-rules any external set of rules. It is those who are seeking integrity through action, regardless of the constraints society, politics or parents impose, who drive the plays.

37

3:   Falstaff.

*A goodly portly man, i' faith, and a corpulent;
of a cheerful look, a pleasing eye, and a most noble
carriage... I see virtue in his looks. If then the tree may
be known by the fruit, as the fruit by the tree, then,
peremptorily I speak it, there is virtue in that Falstaff.*

Falstaff's description of himself

*That trunk of humours, that bolting hutch of beastliness,
that swoll'n parcel of dropsies, that huge bombard of
sack, that stuff'd cloakbag of guts, that roasted
Manningtree ox with the pudding in his belly, that
reverend vice, that grey iniquity, that father ruffian, that
vanity in years? Wherein is he good, but to taste sack
and drink it? Wherein neat and cleanly, but to carve a
capon and eat it? Wherein cunning, but in craft?
Wherein crafty, but in villainy?*

Prince Hal's description of Falstaff

- both descriptions from Henry IV Part 1, Act II scene iv

Of all the living, life-loving people whom Shakespeare
creates, the most rounded, filled in and complete is Sir John
Falstaff. His behaviour has attracted acclaim and condemnation
in passionate terms over three hundred years – as if judgement
upon it was a moral necessity. But can we condemn someone so
attractive, and so entertaining? Or approve anyone who cheats
and lies and steals as he does?

The problem is that his anarchy and cynicism matches our
own weary observation of politics and law in the real world: in
such times living on your wits and avoiding all responsibility is an
attractive option. And if his actions result in the humiliation of
authority – rather as a pile of crashed police cars brings a smile to
our faces watching a comedy gangster movie – who will deny us
the laughter?

38

But... "that grey iniquity, that father ruffian".... How can we defend him? Righteous critics, careful school teachers, and all the self-respecting people he bumps up against in the plays, are – very reasonably - appalled by his behaviour. We can easily muster evidence to disown him.

As does his friend Prince Hal on the day that he is crowned King Henry the Fifth.

What are the equations between humour and respect, indulgence and duty, delight and guilt, which *ought* to hold sway over us? *Should* persuasive mirth be allowed to cloud judgement? "Yes" shouts the eager teenager in all of us – "No" insists the nervous parent and the responsible observer of the pain and damage caused by mayhem.

But 'ought' and 'should' do not belong in Shakespeare's theatre. The mirror he wishes to hold in front of us will reflect back things as they are – not as the moral policewoman might wish them to be. The dilemmas set up by Falstaff's behaviour give us the stuff of drama – and the stuff of life.

Add to this what actors and audiences *know*: Falstaff is most lovable, entertaining, intriguing, right-thinking, witty, truthful (- yes, **truthful**!), benevolent.... Well – he lies, he steals, he fails to pay bills or pay back loans, he's a promise breaker, a glutton, a coward.... we agree.... But his heart is open and warm, his intelligence never amiss. He is no fool.

And he is very funny - often at his own expense.

Let us observe Falstaff in action. Here are some extracts from a scene in **Henry IV Part Two** - the second of the three plays which present the youth and kingship of King Henry the Fifth.

The Prince has recently struck the Lord Chief Justice on the ear (if evidence of his abominable behaviour is needed, there it is). Civil war threatens – the King recruits forces. Sir John Falstaff will be raising troops to join him, as he did at previous skirmishes [this is one of the obligations of a knight: to provide soldiers for his King]. It is regarding the recent Gadshill robbery, which indeed (we know) did involve him, that the Justice has been trying to summons Sir John.

Enter the LORD CHIEF JUSTICE and his SERVANT.

*PAGE.   Sir, here comes the nobleman that committed the
         Prince for striking him about Bardolph.*

FALSTAFF.   Wait close; I will not see him.

CHIEF JUSTICE.   What's he that goes there?

SERVANT.   Falstaff, an't please your lordship.

CHIEF JUSTICE.   He that was in question for the robb'ry?

*SERVANT.   He, my lord; but he hath since done good
           service at Shrewsbury, and, as I hear, is now going
           with some charge to the Lord John of Lancaster.*

[John of Lancaster is Prince Hal's brother]

CHIEF JUSTICE.   What, to York? Call him back again.

SERVANT.   Sir John Falstaff!

FALSTAFF.   Boy, tell him I am deaf.

PAGE.   You must speak louder; my master is deaf.

*CHIEF JUSTICE.   I am sure he is, to the hearing of
                anything good. Go, pluck him by the elbow; I
                must speak with him.*

SERVANT.   Sir John!

… he approaches Falstaff, provoking the following attack:

*FALSTAFF.   What! a young knave, and begging! Is there
            not wars? Is   there not employment? Doth not the
            King lack subjects? Do not the rebels need soldiers?
            Though it be a shame to be on any side but one, it
            is worse shame to beg than to be on the worst side,
            were it worse than the name of rebellion can tell
            how to make it.*

SERVANT.   You mistake me, sir.

40

FALSTAFF.   Why, sir, did I say you were an honest man? Setting my knighthood and my soldiership aside, I had lied in my throat if I had said so.

.....and so on, until the moment when the Lord Chief Justice finally gets his attention, and Falstaff is amazed to see him there:

CHIEF JUSTICE.   Sir John Falstaff, a word with you.

FALSTAFF.   My good lord! God give your lordship good time of day. I am glad to see your lordship abroad. I heard say your lordship was sick; I hope your lordship goes abroad by advice. Your lordship, though not clean past your youth, hath yet some smack of age in you, some relish of the saltness of time; and I most humbly beseech your lordship to have a reverend care of your health.

CHIEF JUSTICE.   Sir John, I sent for you before your expedition to Shrewsbury.

FALSTAFF.   An't please your lordship, I hear his Majesty is return'd with some discomfort from Wales.

CHIEF JUSTICE.   I talk not of his Majesty. You would not come when I sent for you.

FALSTAFF.   And I hear, moreover, his Highness is fall'n into this same whoreson apoplexy.

CHIEF JUSTICE.   Well God mend him! I pray you let me speak with you.

FALSTAFF.   This apoplexy, as I take it, is a kind of lethargy, an't please your lordship, a kind of sleeping in the blood, a whoreson tingling.

CHIEF JUSTICE.   What tell you me of it? Be it as it is.

FALSTAFF.   It hath it original from much grief, from study, and perturbation of the brain. I have read the cause of his effects in Galen; it is a kind of deafness.

41

CHIEF JUSTICE. I think you are fall'n into the disease,
for you hear not what I say to you.

FALSTAFF. Very well, my lord, very well. Rather an't
please you, it is the disease of not listening, the
malady of not marking, that I am troubled withal.

.... and a bit more until:

CHIEF JUSTICE. I sent for you, when there were
matters against you for your life, to come speak
with me.

FALSTAFF. As I was then advis'd by my learned counsel
in the laws of this land-service, I did not come.

From Henry IV Part 2   I ii

Is not this honest? To admit that he didn't hear because he
refused to listen and didn't attend the summons because he has
taken legal advice that if he did he might be in trouble. He admits
these things to the very man who has the power to imprison or fine
him – if he can get him to court. This is sophisticated anarchy.
Seeing authority confused and defeated in this way awakes
childish joy in us.

Note that it is Falstaff who steers the conversation to
deafness. And he enquires after the Justice's health, teasingly, but
with a veneer of polished politeness that, as the conversation
continues, almost flatters the Justice into believing in Falstaff's
sincerity: so the moment comes when, referring to the expedition
against the rebels with Prince John of Lancaster, he says:

CHIEF JUSTICE.   Well, be honest, be honest, and God
bless your expedition.

.... which remark Falstaff seizes upon to ask:

FALSTAFF.   Will your lordship lend me a thousands pound to
furnish me forth?

42

How should the Lord Chief Justice respond to that? Surely even *he* will laugh – won over by the sheer audacity of wit and roguery. Unless he has not an ounce of sympathy in him.

We have to admit that what Falstaff says about himself at the very beginning of this scene, is true:

> *Man is not able to invent anything that intends to laughter*
> *more than I invent or is invented on me. I am not only witty*
> *in myself, but the cause that wit is in other men.*

Henry IV Part 2   I   ii   7 - 9

How does he do it? Having had no time to draw breath since we started to quote Sir John's words, let us look back at his syntax and train of thought.

It is indeed like a train, with each carriage linked to the next, travelling at breakneck speed through a passionate landscape of body, brain, disease, food and drink. His colourful, leaping logic rushes on past expected termini dumping us in bewilderment: which also happens to characters in the plays, such as Mistress Quickly who publicly attacks him for breach of promise (of marriage) but has hardly paused for breath before he has won her over - and suggested that she pawn her tapestries to raise cash (for him) [**Henry IV part 2   II   i**]. His highly intelligent manipulation of conversation finds an echo in the artistry of his vocabulary, knitted into amazing cadences: *Sleeping in the blood...   Some smack of age... Some relish of the saltness of time... Setting my knighthood and my soldiership aside...   Worse shame to beg than to be on the worst side.* Take any phrase and roll it round the tongue. Try out each speech with variation of emphasis, pause and inflexion: it never fails you – there are a thousand ways to speak it, and fathoming the intelligence behind it would take a thousand years.

One of the remarkable skills that Shakespeare has is the creation of character through the words that each one speaks. No extra information is needed by the actor who plays Falstaff other than the words he utters. No back- story, no historical research, is necessary to flesh out this person: in the speaking of the word the 'character' comes to life.

Nothing will illustrate this more clearly than contrasting the speeches from the previous pages with a speech by Hal's father. Here, Bolingbroke, newly crowned King Henry IV (having deposed King Richard II) laments the behaviour of his son. This is the first mention of Prince Hal in the sequence of plays [*Rich II, Henry IV & V*].

> *Can no man tell me of my unthrifty son?*
> *'Tis full three months since I did see him last.*
> *If any plague hang over us, 'tis he.*
> *I would to God, my lords, he might be found.*
> *Inquire at London, 'mongst the taverns there,*
> *For there, they say, he daily doth frequent*
> *With unrestrained loose companions,*
> *Even such, they say, as stand in narrow lanes*
> *And beat our watch and rob our passengers,*
> *Which he, young wanton and effeminate boy,*
> *Takes on the point of honour to support*
> *So dissolute a crew.*
>
> **Richard II V iii 1 – 12**

This speech is clearly placed here to prepare us for the next (three) plays in which Hal will appear, but it also fills out the character of Henry IV, who up to now has, on his journey to become king, presented a more aggressive front. With Falstaff's words and rhythms ringing in our heads, we need not wonder that the prince prefers conversations with Falstaff to being at the court. There is nothing "unrestrained" or "loose" about *this* speech – those words are reserved for the "effeminate" boy who is a "plague". Well, it is plain speaking – calling upon God, claiming the common touch ("*they* say"), inviting confidences ("can no man tell me…"). At the same time we have the strong, new king revealing his concern for his public image, the future inheritance in the lineal descent of the crown to his son, and his personal dismay. How Hal manages to readjust his father's perception is one of the main themes of these plays – step by step the dramatic pattern alters.

- - - - -

Aside. Interestingly, in the next few lines which follow this speech in *Richard II*, Henry IV speaks with two other young men: Percy, known as Hotspur, the son of Northumberland and later a rebel, and Aumerle, who rushes in, desperately pleading to be excused his near involvement in an assassination attempt. Are these two potential traitors meant to be contrasted with this "wanton" son who, *we* know (because he's due to become Henry V), will in fact be loyal and heroic.

- - - - -

The stories of the "unthrifty" behaviour of this "wanton" [= capricious, unrestrained] prince are part of the folklore which attached to King Henry the Fifth within a few years of his death. His father's lament quoted above gives us the essence of these stories. Falstaff does not appear in them.

In the literature and folklore of every nation there exist outstanding figures who become emblems of glory. Some, such as Alexander the Great or King David of Jerusalem, become symbols of heroic achievement for whole civilisations. Others such as King Arthur, George Washington or Garibaldi remain identified with one nation as saviour or founding father.

Such a hero was King Henry the Fifth for England. His tomb in the Abbey at Westminster, on the River Thames not far from the City (of London), was for centuries an attraction for pilgrims – as it is now for tourists. Not only was he a glorious patriotic figure for the Elizabethans: he returned to England in 1943 at a time of national emergency, promoted by Laurence Olivier's film of Shakespeare's play *Henry V*.

This is the King who was Prince Hal.

What is the true education for a Prince – or rather, in myth and legend, what sort of tutor prepares a King to take power?

45

The answer has little connection to morality. From Hermes to Merlin (advisor to King Arthur) ... through Silenos (tutor to the Greek God Dionysos) and Beelzebub (in English Morality plays of the medieval times).... figures appear who teach princes the cunning and trickery which politics demands – along with tainting them with the ways of traitors and criminals so that they *know* not from books but from experience the ways of the world. At the moment of putting on the crown many of these tales have the new king put this tutor to death. Now "the King" is alone; now the King is heroic, just, merciful, a great warrior, an accomplished diplomat. And the debt he owes to his youthful mentor is cancelled and forgotten.

Such a figure is Falstaff. However much we are ashamed by Hal's denial of him when the day of coronation arrives [the final scene of *Henry IV part 2*] we have to admit: there is no choice.

Perhaps the strongest demonstration of the glory of Falstaff and the joy experienced in his company, are the major works of other artists who have made use of him. Orson Welles acted in his own film "Chimes at Midnight"; Verdi wrote an Opera; and Robert Nye wrote a novel called "Falstaff" in which the old man dictates his autobiography to a not-always-compliant scribe - he does not die before Agincourt but gives his account of that battle and the behaviour of the king, having started his adventurous and sexually active life as a pageboy.

And what seems beyond question is that Falstaff holds a special place in the affection of his creator – even to his name: surely there is some peculiar interconnection between "Fall Staff" and "Shake Spear".

4 : The Pageboy

I am almost afraid to stand alone

Romeo and Juliet V iii 10

Standing alone is not an unusual experience for a major character in a Shakespeare play. Kent and Edgar in *King Lear*, Hamlet, Juliet, and many of the Kings whose plays take their names, live in an almost-defining state in which they 'alone' must struggle with decisions and emotions forced upon them by events - situations in which there is no possibility of a friend's advice or some 'other' objective point of view. It may be that this need for self-reliance and self-belief is an aspect of mature humanity that Shakespeare wishes us to acknowledge.

But the quotation above is spoken not by a major actor in a play but by a boy who speaks only nine lines in the final act of *Romeo and Juliet.*

He is pageboy to Count Paris.

- - - - -

Aside. A pageboy might be only 7 years old when first taking up his role in medieval times. He was probably the son of an aristocratic family, himself destined to become a knight when he gained adulthood. His residence, which might last up to 7 years, would establish social and political alliance between the families, and give him valuable lessons in traditions and manners.

- - - - -

Paris is the husband that Juliet's father has selected for her. But she, being already secretly married to Romeo, resorts to desperate means to avoid the wedding – a drug supplied to her by Friar Laurence.

47

One of the wonders of Shakespeare the poet is how he gives us the play in our imagination as well us on the stage. The vivid description of how this drug works and the explanation of funeral arrangements in the city of Verona – where noble bodies are laid out in the cool, dry family vault un-coffined – is a small drama in itself as given to us by Friar Laurence:

> *Take thou this vial, being then in bed,*
> *And this distilled liquor drink thou off;*
> *When presently through all thy veins shall run*
> *A cold and drowsy humour; for no pulse*
> *Shall keep his native progress, but surcease;*
> *No warmth, no breath, shall testify thou livest;*
> *The roses in thy lips and cheeks shall fade*
> *To paly ashes, thy eyes' windows fall*
> *Like death when he shuts up the day of life;*
> *Each part, depriv'd of supple government,*
> *Shall, stiff and stark and cold, appear like death;*
> *And in this borrowed likeness of shrunk death*
> *Thou shalt continue two-and-forty hours,*
> *And then awake as from a pleasant sleep.*
> *Now, when the bridegroom in the morning comes*
> *To rouse thee from thy bed, there art thou dead.*
> *Then, as the manner of our country is,*
> *In thy best robes uncovered on the bier*
> *Thou shalt be borne to that same ancient vault*
> *Where all the kindred of the Capulets lie.*
> *In the mean time, against thou shalt awake,*
> *Shall Romeo, by my letters, know our drift*
> *And hither shall he come; and he and I*
> *Will watch thy waking… …..*

Romeo and Juliet IV i 93 - 114

Here are we told of the custom whereby "the bridegroom in the morning comes" to wake the bride on her wedding day. And so it is that Paris comes [Act IV scene v] and finds Juliet apparently dead. It is possible that his pageboy accompanies Paris in this scene and in others before this, but he does not speak until **Act V**

48

Scene iii which is set in the churchyard *and* inside the "ancient vault where all the kindred of the Capulets lie" which is referred to several times in the play as "the monument".

Quite how to stage the churchyard and the monument presents some problems for a director. When Romeo arrives his first words (to his servant Balthasar) are "give me the mattock and the wrenching iron": he is going to break open the locked gate of the monument – therefore we need the gate, the inside of the monument, *and* the open space of the churchyard - all to be on stage. The scene opens with the arrival of Paris with the pageboy.

> *PARIS.   Give me thy torch, boy. Hence, and stand aloof.*
> *Yet put it out, for I would not be seen.*
> *Under yond yew tree lay thee all along,*
> *Holding thine ear close to the hollow ground.*
> *So shall no foot upon the churchyard tread*
> *(Being loose, unfirm, with digging up of graves)*
> *But thou shalt hear it. Whistle then to me,*
> *As signal that thou hear'st something approach.*
> *Give me those flowers.   Do as I bid thee, go.*

> **Romeo and Juliet V iii 1 - 9**

Shakespeare's stage, having no scenery, requires that we are told exactly where we are – hence the words "churchyard", "graves" and "yew trees" in the first words of the scene.

Paris has arrived with a burning torch and flowers – both carried by the pageboy. No wrenching iron. He intends to lay the flowers by the gate of the monument and stay to weep and pray.

The pageboy, having obeyed the instruction to put out the torch, gives Paris the flowers, moves away and speaks the first two of his nine lines:

> *PAGEBOY.   I am almost afraid to stand alone*
> *Here in the churchyard; yet I will adventure.*

49

Immediately we recognise this boy: accustomed to do as he is told, his duty overcomes his anxiety. That "almost" is the debate in his mind – refusing to allow fear its mastery – and that "yet I will" is his brave determination.

His words, spoken to nobody but the audience, give us an immediate connection to the scene: he is one of us, watching what goes on as well as taking part. Very soon he hears Romeo coming and gives that whistle.

Paris is alarmed:

> *What cursed foot wanders this way tonight*
> *To cross my obsequies and true love's rite?*
> *What, with a torch? Muffle me, night, awhile.*

This torch is also not carried by Romeo but by his servant, along with the mattock and wrenching iron. These he takes – and in exchange gives Balthasar a letter for his father and the instructions to "be gone" (along with fierce threats of violent attack if he were to stay and "pry" into Romeo's action).

- - - - -

Aside. Balthasar does not go away. He remains in the churchyard and apparently falls asleep – woken by Friar Laurence hurrying to reach Juliet before she wakes. The Friar is too late: that is to say too late to stop Romeo who, finding Juliet apparently dead, has drunk his poison. Friar Laurence tries to get Juliet to come away but she refuses and he, terrified by the consequences of all he has done, hurries away, deserting her. He is the fourth person to do so, following her father, her mother and the nurse. In one sense Romeo should be added to this list as he deserts her by dying: but the opposite sense is more true – Romeo has planned to die in order that he shall not desert her but be with her in death.

- - - - -

50

When Paris sees Romeo forcing the gate he is appalled. This is "that banished haughty Montague" who killed Tybalt and has come to desecrate the tomb. He steps forward to challenge Romeo who, although he doesn't know who it is, says....

> *I beseech thee, youth,*
> *Put not another sin upon my head*
> *By urging me to fury...*

But he is quickly "urged" to fury and fights back when Paris draws his sword. Witnessing this the pageboy speaks his third line:

> *O Lord, they fight! I will go call the watch.*

"The watch". He means of course the watchmen who patrol the streets of the town by night. We heard of them before, when Romeo, under sentence of banishment, was advised by the Friar to leave Verona "before the watch be set" [he didn't: he spent the night with Juliet] - presumably because the city gates are shut at night and the watchmen guard them.

But the word 'watch' occurs also in the play with other meaning. So, when he goes to Capulet's party and spots Juliet, Romeo says "I'll watch her place of stand" [I v 50] and in the instructions given to Juliet by the Friar and quoted earlier, he says "he and I will watch thy waking".

Thinking of these two uses of the word "watch" we realise that the word contains a sense of expectation. Romeo is bewitched by the sight of Juliet and focuses his attention in order to find out – and indeed plan - what will happen next. A similar sense possesses that moment when Romeo and the Friar "watch" Juliet, waiting for her to wake. Alas, this moment never comes. But our "watching" of the play is likewise full of expectation: the letters sent to Romeo by the Friar do not reach him, the wedding to Paris is brought forward by a day .... The catastrophe might be avoided if only... if only....

A couple of pages ago I remarked that we in the audience were "watching" with the pageboy. Using that word with its Shakespeare implication is appropriate. When used today, the word lacks urgency – it has become more passive in meaning, the sense of expectation has been lost. This is what happens to language over time: words tend to diminish in specific-ness.

- - - - -

Aside. This tendency is powerfully illustrated by the word "presently" which in Shakespeare's day meant (of course) instantly/now/at once/immediately and has been dumbed down to mean 'soon' .

- - - - -

We might question whether Shakespeare deliberately planted the word "watch" through the play [it occurs more than a dozen times in various forms] as though to urge us on to see – to hope – to fear – to partake of the drama: "watch !" Some support for such an idea might be claimed from a slightly absurd little scene inserted into **Act IV**. Juliet is due to be married the next day and Lord Capulet decides to stay up and help prepare the feast – much to the scorn of the Nurse:

> NURSE.   *Go, you cot-quean, go,*
> *Get you to bed! Faith, you'll be sick to-morrow*
> *For this night's watching.*
> CAPULET. *No, not a whit. What, I have watch'd ere now*
> *All night for lesser cause, and ne'er been sick.*
> LADY C.   *Ay, you have been a mouse-hunt in your time;*
> *But I will watch you from such watching now.*
> CAPULET. *A jealous hood, a jealous hood!*

Romeo and Juliet IV iv 6 - 13

... and the scene continues with some comic coming and going of servants preparing the food - light relief preceding the scene in which Juliet will be found apparently dead - linked in to the play with this extra, strange use of the word "watch".

The final scene of *Romeo and Juliet* contains a great deal of activity. Some we have already observed – the arrival of Paris and the Pageboy, and Romeo and his servant, and the fight, and the flight of the boy. But there is much more.

The pageboy arrives with the watchmen:

> *PAGEBOY. This is the place, there where the torch doth burn.*

- - - - -

Aside. That torch, inside the monument, was placed by Romeo so that he could see Juliet, and continues to burn. It was seen by Friar Laurence when he arrived....

> *What torch is yond that vainly lends his light*
> *To grubs and eyeless skulls? As I discern*
> *It burneth in the Capel's monument.*

> **Romeo & Juliet   V   iii   124 - 126**

The word "torch" has occurred four times in this scene. But it was planted in our ears and linked to Juliet way back at the beginning of the play so that, like the word "watch", it carries other implications with it. When he and his friends were on the way to the Capulet's party at which he will set eyes on Juliet, Romeo calls out: "Give me a torch" – as if he knows he needs some aid to see what he will see. And indeed, when he does see her:

> *Oh, she doth teach the torches to burn bright.*

> **Romeo & Juliet   I   v   44**

- - - - -

There are at least three watchmen. They search the churchyard and the monument, they find Balthasar and the bodies of Paris and Romeo and "Juliet bleeding, warm and newly dead." They run back to the town...

> *Go tell the Prince, run to the Capulets,*
> *Raise up the Montagues....*

53

... and one of them (written into the Folio as "3 Wat.") returns with Friar Laurence who fled when Juliet refused to leave the monument with him. She stayed with her dead Romeo (who had drunk his poison when he found her 'dead') but Laurence was overcome by panic, his plans destroyed, the dread of responsibility for what he had done in marrying them, all too much for him, so that even when the watchmen find him he....

> *... trembles, sighs and weeps.*
> *We took this mattock and this spade from him*
> *As he was coming from the church-yard side.*

Soon the Prince arrives, and Capulet, and Lady Capulet who says:

> *The people in the street cry 'Romeo',*
> *Some 'Juliet', and some 'Paris', and all run*
> *With open outcry toward our monument.*

The last person to arrive is Romeo's father, Lord Montague, whose first words bring all to a halt.

> *Alas, my liege, my wife is dead tonight.*
> *Grief of my son's exile hath stopped her breath.*
> *What further woe conspires against mine age?*
> PRINCE. *Look and thou shalt see.*

He looks. His son lies dead. And Juliet dead beside him.

Some forty lines of passionate activity, actual and reported action, noise and movement, have filled the stage since the pageboy entered with the watchmen. It is as if the passion of the now dead lovers, possesses instead the people of Verona. The terrible tragedy of the deaths of Romeo and Juliet is held in a kind of suspended emotional turmoil, not possible to be attended until the chaos has settled down. When it does, we stop and look with Romeo's father at the bodies of his son and Juliet.

- - - - -

Aside.   Sadly, many modern productions edit away
most of this activity – and also the final explanations that
round out the play. Whether this is because the play is
too long [quite a bit more than the "two hours passage of
our play" that we were promised in the prologue] or
because directors believe that there will be more impact
if they focus on the two lovers and leave out the
watchmen and the parental contributions [and even,
sometimes, the Friar's coming to the tomb] is hard to
determine. My claim would be that Shakespeare knew
how to do it: the extended activity and long speeches
that make up this scene emphasise, replay and put into
context the main event. The shock of the terrible,
unnecessary dying increases with the running in and out
and the shouting. The full impact of the reason for, and
the possible preventability of the tragedy are allowed full
rein.

- - - - -

The Prince takes charge and demands explanations. Friar
Laurence, Balthasar, and finally our pageboy, speak.

> *PRINCE.*   *Sirrah, what made your master in this place?*
>
> *PAGEBOY.* *He came with flowers to strew his lady's grave;*
> *And bid me stand aloof, and so I did.*
> ope=open   *Anon comes one with light to ope the tomb;*
> *And by-and-by my master drew on him;*
> *And then I ran away to call the watch.*
>
> **Romeo and Juliet V iii 281 – 285**

From the flowers – it was he that carried them to the
graveyard (*"Give me those flowers" PARIS*) - to the calling of the
watchman, he tells it. His loyalty and sense of duty are matched
by his truthful simplicity. We have 'watched' some hours as the
tragedy unfolded: this boy has seen a tiny piece of the action. But

55

what a seeing! Through him the whole play is given another dimension – it is seen from a new vantage point. And for him? What burns into his mind that night will shape his world for ever. One day he will be able to ponder the full story – a story that has become famous in his city as it has in our world as history, legend, art, and myth.

But just now this child - in awe of the Prince and the terror of the place - speaks out clearly. And more than that: he gives us a commentary on the action of the play.

Printed copies of the play begin with a prologue in which the outcome of the play – the death of Romeo and Juliet – is revealed: though this prologue is actually omitted in the Folio of 1623. This sonnet length speech describes ...

> ...*their parents' rage,*
> *Which, but their children's end, naught could remove.*

This is the 'rage' of *Sonnet 65* – death and destruction, against which we have so little hope:

> *How with this rage shall beauty hold a plea,*
> *Whose action is no stronger than a flower.*

The play ends, indeed, with the 'removal' of the 'rage': the fathers join hands [an echo of the first meeting of the lovers?] and speak of their intent to raise statues of the pair in remembrance and reconciliation: "Poor sacrifices of our enmity". So too the sonnet ends with the hope that poetry might, through remembrance and imagination, produce "this miracle":

> *That in black ink my love may still shine bright.*

Now at the end of the play, we recall:

> *PARIS.   Give me thy torch, boy. Hence, and stand aloof.*
> *Yet put it out, for I would not be seen.*

He did as he was told – this boy. The torch was not given to Paris, but it was extinguished. The light was out. But, now he tells us, a few moments later...

56

Anon comes one with light to ope the tomb.

This is Romeo. With light. To open the tomb. To bring light to death. To bring... the pageboy might have said:

*Anon comes one with **love** to ope the tomb.*

Or rather, in the poetry of the moment, that *is* what is said – and it is the child's voice that says it. Death. Light. Love – to heal the terrible hate between the families, this was the only way, as we were told in the Prologue.

We have spent more than "two hours" enthralled by the "toil" of the actors – not least by our brave pageboy, "almost afraid" yet determined to "adventure", in order to give us the whole play in one line:

Anon comes one with light to ope the tomb.

To find so much in a 'minor' character – the realised individual, the being-us watcher, the symbolism in his speech and action, his gift to us of one line to sum up the play – is not to make an interpretation beyond Shakespeare's intention: it is an integral aspect of the poetry. This play, *Romeo and Juliet*, is the very peak of accomplishment, the perfection of the 'poetic drama' – that mode of theatre which the Elizabethan poet/playwrights invented. Never again did Shakespeare create such another so-perfect piece. Indeed we might suspect that having achieved this – alongside *A Midsummer Night's Dream* and *Richard II*, which also qualify as master-works of the genre – Shakespeare had achieved his ambition and might, had he not then set out to develop his art in new directions, retired with honour.

Much joy may be experienced in the digging out of some of the artifice of this - and all the other – plays. The signposts delivered by the words "torch" and "watch" in this piece, and the marvellously dramatic, focussed speech that Friar Laurence delivers to Juliet when giving her the potion, prompt us to be alert to such devices in the plays. The overall construction of the play creates what is virtually a single, long 'poem': to think of it in musical terms - as a symphony, or, more appropriately, an oratorio - is one way of imagining this. Such is the skill of telling, retelling, and placing into our minds the images and recollections of events and actions , that our memory of the play may well contain 'imagined' episodes which are not there - not in the script, nor in the enactment of it, but imagined from listening to the words.

- - - - -

> **Aside**. Such a recollection may be that of witnessing the procession in which Juliet "in thy best robes uncovered on the bier" is borne to the monument. Could it be from a film, or a ballet? Hardly from a stage production. Was it only the Friar's description of it which created this memory?

- - - - -

The wholeness and comprehensive totality of this play [and the other two mentioned above from roughly the same date of composition] is achieved again in *Macbeth, The Tempest* and *Twelfth Night* – albeit they are very different sorts of plays, from this and from each other. Alongside these there are 20 other plays after *Romeo and Juliet*. Full of invention and novelty none of them lacks brilliance: Shakespeare is breaking the bounds of the 'complete poem', writing plays which are not self-contained and deliberately invite us to broader and undefined worlds. The most extreme, unfettered, endlessly ungraspable and question raising, is, of course, *Hamlet*.

5: Imagination

HIPPOLYTA. This is the silliest stuff that ever I heard.

THESEUS. The best in this kind are but shadows; and the worst are no worse, if imagination amend them.

HIPPOLYTA. It must be your imagination then, and not theirs.

Midsummer Night's Deam   V i 207 - 210

On our journey to meet Hamlet and note his advice to the actors we should consider what Shakespeare has to say about theatre in previous plays.

Written about the same time as **Romeo and Juliet**, **Midsummer Night's Dream** was – and remains – one of the most extraordinary pieces of theatre ever conceived. It is about love, marriage, magic, dream, and acting, and is one of the four plays – the others being **Macbeth**, **The Tempest** and **Hamlet** itself – in which the spirit world is directly represented and its impact upon the material and the everyday, fundamental to the plot. The movement in and out of magic and dream and theatre is both specific and subtly shifted so that at times we are suspended in undefined realms: at, for example, the moment when the prankster spirit, Puck, rescues Bottom from his enchantment by pulling off his donkey's head – a simple theatrical action reversing what was a powerful magical transformation.

The first and last Acts of the play take place in Athens, mainly in the court; the three central Acts in "a wood outside Athens" which turns out to be inhabited by medieval English spirits.   To this wood go two pairs of lovers, escaping the law, pursuing each other; a group of working men who are rehearsing a play; and a hunting party including the duke of Athens, Theseus, and his bride Hippolyta.   These two celebrated characters from Greek Mythology are written into the play in such a way that the actors who play them can double up to play the King and Queen of fairyland, Oberon and Titania. The balance between the four groups of characters – the workmen, the spirits, the lovers and the royals – is beautifully balanced in the construction of the play. So much so that we might question who is the protagonist?

- - - - -

Aside. Protagonist: the character whose actions and decisions drive the plot. Most obvious if named in the title of the play – *Macbeth, Hamlet.*

- - - - -

When, in the final Act, the play of *Pyramus and Thisbe* [a play with two protagonist like *Romeo and Juliet, Antony and Cleopatra*] is enthusiastically presented at court by those...

> *Hard-handed men that work in Athens here,*
> *Which never labourr'd in their minds till now.*
>
> **Midsummer Night's Deam   V i 72 - 73**

... the Duke, his new wife, the reconciled lovers and others in the court, become the audience – they join us. Or do we join them – as guests at the court to watch their bit of theatre? Who are the players? Who the spectators? Are some – or all – of us bit-players in the production?

The shift of 'reality' into dream and theatre is rounded out at the very end of the performance by Puck speaking directly and finally to us:

> *If we shadows have offended,*
> *Think but this, and all is mended,*
> *That you have but slumb'red here*
> *While these visions did appear,*
> *And this weak and idle theme,*
> *No more yielding but a dream.*
>
> **Midsummer Night's Deam   V i 409 - 414**

Puck's description of himself and his fellow actors as "shadows" picks up Theseus's reply to Hippolyta's complaint about the performance of the workers' play – that it is "the silliest stuff":

THESEUS. The best in this kind are but shadows.

'Shadow' is a word Shakespeare often employs – especially in his early plays. 'Shadow' is the alternative to 'Substance'. This is from *Titus Andronicus* [perhaps his first surviving play] when Titus himself, driven almost mad by grief and anger, acts out a furious attack upon a fly - his brother speaks:

Alas, poor man! Grief has so wrought on him,
He takes false shadows for true substances.
Titus Andronicus III ii 79-80

Shadows may be 'false' but they have their uses. In another early play, *Two Gentlemen of Verona,* a young man bemoaning the absence of his beloved, expresses his loss:

What joy is joy, if Silvia be not by?
Unless it be to think that she is by,
And feed upon the shadow of perfection.
Two Gentlemen of Verona III i 175 -177

This clever image is a beautiful illustration of the process of recall and amorous indulgence. If he can hold the idea strongly enough to "feed upon" it, the thought of Silvia becomes tangible – though elusive: an echo, a memory, insubstantial. This baffling, transitory quality gives to the word "shadow" a quality of ungraspable-ness.

A most interesting dispute about reality, substance and shadow, occurs in the first part of the three-play history of *Henry VI* - another early play. The brave English warrior Talbot has been taken prisoner by the Countess of Auvergne – or so it seems. She gloats that she now has him – he is 'substance' where before he was only a 'shadow':

COUNTESS. *Long time thy shadow hath been thrall to me,*
For in my gallery thy picture hangs;
But now the substance shall endure the like
And I will chain these legs and arms of thine
That hast by tyranny these many years
Wasted our country, slain our citizens,
And sent our sons and husbands captive.
TALBOT. *Ha, ha, ha!*
COUNTESS. *Laughest thou, wretch? Thy mirth shall turn to moan.*
TALBOT. *I laugh to see your ladyship so fond*
To think that you have aught but Talbot's shadow
Whereon to practise your severity.
COUNTESS. *Why, art not thou the man?*
TALBOT. *I am indeed.*
COUNTESS. *Then have I substance too.*
TALBOT. *No, no, I am but shadow of myself.*
You are deceiv'd, my substance is not here;
For what you see is but the smallest part
And least proportion of humanity.
I tell you, madam, were the whole frame here,
It is of such a spacious lofty pitch
Your roof were not sufficient to contain 't.
COUNTESS. *This is a riddling merchant for the nonce;*
He will be here, and yet he is not here.
How can these contrarieties agree?
TALBOT. *That will I show you presently.*
                    Enter soldiers

How say you, madam? Are you now persuaded
That Talbot is but shadow of himself?
These are his substance......

Henry VI Pt I   II iii 36 - 63

... and she is forced to entertain him as her guest rather than her prisoner. Two things may be noted about this lengthy exchange. Firstly, the ease of flowing language, quite simple to frame on the tongue and very matter-of-fact (rather than matter of symbolism). And secondly it is almost as though the unnecessary extension of the scene [it continues for another 20 lines] is nothing more than a frame for this debate about Shadow and Substance.

Not all Shakespeare's warriors are as straightforward as Talbot. King Henry IV, fighting a civil war,has a number of his knights pretend to be him, dressed in "his colours". The famous, brave Scottish Douglas, meeting him, cries out:

> *Another King? They grow like Hydra's heads!*
> *I am the Douglas, fatal to all those*
> *That wear those colours on them. What art thou*
> *That counterfeit'st the person of a king?*

The real man, the real king, replies:

> *The king himself, who, Douglas, grieves at heart*
> *So many of his shadows thou hast met*
> *And not the very king.*

Henry IV Pt I   V iv 24 - 30

It is noticeable that since that first use of the word in *Titus Andronicus*, all these quoted 'shadows' have been people. In later plays the word is used more generally, but all those first images come forcefully back to mind in *Macbeth* and *King Lear* [much later plays, after *Hamlet*, ten years after *Midsummer Night's Dream*] as deep and poignant images. Insulted and rejected by his daughter Goneril, Lear asks who it is he has become since he lost his authority. The Fool replies:

> *Lear's shadow.*

King Lear I iv 228

And the full theatrical shadow world of meaning and action reappears at Macbeth's darkest moment:

> *Out, out, brief candle!*
> *Life's but a walking shadow, a poor player*
> *That struts and frets his hour upon the stage*
> *And then is heard no more.*

Macbeth V v 23 - 26

These subtle variations in context and meaning demonstrate how careful we must be before we use the Glossary to 'look up the meaning' of any word which stalks its way through Shakespeare's plays. Rather than academic resolution we should expect and allow poetic uncertainty, attracted by and delighting in the evasive, provocative variety.

Returning to plays of 1595 there is one more inescapable focus on the 'shadow'. At the centre of the play *Richard II* is the great scene where we witness the deposition of the King. When Richard hands over the crown to Bolingbroke, he asks for a mirror. Looking at himself he remarks that:

A brittle glory shineth in this face.

And then he breaks the mirror! This is the cue for a romantic extension of his image of himself and his situation:

As brittle as the glory is the face;
For there it is, crack'd in a hundred shivers.
Mark, silent king, the moral of this sport -
How soon my sorrow hath destroy'd my face.

But Bolingbroke, the "silent king" – whom we must now call Henry IV - will have nothing to do with that:

HENRY. The shadow of your sorrow hath destroy'd
*   The shadow of your face.*

RICHARD.   Say that again.
*   The shadow of my sorrow? Ha! let's see.*
*   'Tis very true: my grief lies all within;*
*   And these external manner of laments*
*   Are merely shadows to the unseen grief*
*   That swells with silence in the tortur'd soul.*
*   There lies the substance.*

Richard II IV i 287 - 298

Substance again: the real thing - the opposite of Shadow. And "There" lies the substance – but where? Why, in the "tortured soul". And all his lamentation cannot fully portray this desperate, real thing. So indeed his action and his words have been only "the shadow of my sorrow".

But the actor playing Richard will be tempted at this moment to point at the broken mirror: *there* lies the substance. All his "brittle glory" broken, gone, "crack'd in a hundred shivers" – so much for 'substance'.

But let us reconsider the new King Henry's words which set Richard off on this poetic journey :

> *The shadow of your sorrow hath destroy'd*
> *The shadow of your face.*

Henry is being practical - un-poetic – and has no intention of encouraging the symbolic, romantic, suffering imagery which Richard calls up. In fact Henry's lines are completely scornful of this. The "shadow of your sorrow" is the absurd, histrionic display of all "your" self-centred, pitiful demands for sympathy. You have agreed to this hand-over of the crown and you know that you are doing this because you have not got what it takes to be a king. So it is all to no avail, this performance of sadness – this "shadow of sorrow" - culminating in that final pointless action, breaking the mirror, to destroy the "shadow of your face" – meaning, now, nothing more than 'the reflection of your face in the mirror'.

From this tense English court, we return to the comfort of the Athenian court where Bottom and his friends are performing their play.

> *The best in this kind are but shadows; and the*
> *worst are no worse, if imagination amend them.*

Theseus defends the actors against Hippolyta's criticism – and in doing so he appears to be standing up for art and poetry and theatre. But we must be careful how we interpret these remarks because both Theseus and Hippolyta are inconsistent in their attitude towards imagination – and dream and fantasy. In the present exchange it is Hippolyta who holds back from giving credence to the performance by her remark:

This is the silliest stuff that ever I heard [1]

...and Theseus who wishes to give value to the unsubstantial "shadows" by calling on "imagination".

But earlier – in the interesting exchanges which introduce the final Act of *Midsummer Night's Dream* – it was the other way round. The young lovers' explanation of what happened to them in the dream-wood rather impressed Hippolyta :

> .... *the story of the night told over*
> .... *grows to something of great constancy.*
>
> **Midsummer Night's Deam   V i 23 & 26**

.....whereas Theseus says that he:

> ....*never may believe*
> *These antique fables, nor these fairy toys.*
>
> **Midsummer Night's Deam   V i 2 - 3**

These lines introduce his lengthy put down of "imagination". They are worth quoting in full because, out of context, they are often taken as being in praise of 'poetry' and poets – whereas the intention is to point out how unreliable and akin to madness is "imagination".

Indeed it is the "trick" of "strong imagination" to deceive us. Notice the 'apprehension' and the 'comprehension' – both mentioned in the second and third lines, and again near the end. The 'apprehension' is both what we fear is true and what we wish to be true. This becomes the spur, the excuse, the ingredient of belief, which replaces observation and logic – true 'comprehension' – allowing us deceitfully to think it *is* true.

The recounted experience of the lovers in the wood – all "the story of the night told over" – is what starts him off.

---

[1] She is in good company. On 29 September 1662 Samuel Pepys, oblivious of the fact that he is almost quoting from the play, wrote in his diary "saw *Midsummer Night's Dream* which I had never seen before, nor shall ever again, for it is the most insipid ridiculous play that ever I saw in my life."

Lovers and madmen have such seething brains,
Such shaping fantasies, that apprehend
More than cool reason ever comprehends.
The lunatic, the lover, and the poet,
Are of imagination all compact.
One sees more devils than vast hell can hold;
That is the madman. The lover, all as frantic,
Sees Helen's beauty in a brow of Egypt.
The poet's eye, in a fine frenzy rolling,
Doth glance from heaven to earth, from earth to heaven;
And as imagination bodies forth
The forms of things unknown, the poet's pen
Turns them to shapes, and gives to airy nothing
A local habitation and a name.
Such tricks hath strong imagination,
That if it would but apprehend some joy,
It comprehends some bringer of that joy:
Or, in the night, imagining some fear,
How easy is a bush suppos'd a bear!

Midsummer Night's Dream V i 4-22

The argument may be taken up in a number of ways. Is
the madness of fantastical thinking different from the creative
imagination of the artist? How are we to take this "fine frenzy"
when the poet's eye...

Doth glance from heaven to earth, from earth to heaven. ?

Those of us who wish to support the belief that poetry
might bridge the divide between realms of spiritual reality and the
material world, will immediately seize on this line as evidence in
our favour - and the subsequent lines as accurate description of the
poet's skill: shaping the indescribable truths in words and images.
But if we check back to the madman and the lover we must
understand that each of these active conclusions – the work of
imagination – is a mistaking: the devils do not actually exist, it is a
dark, heavily eye-browed 'gipsy' who is seen to rival Helen of
Troy. And the poet's words are a deceitful description of "airy
nothing". Get real – there are no bears in the garden.

67

But, taking the debate in context, we recognise that not long ago we witnessed some action in which there certainly were, if not bears in the garden, spirits in the wood. Hence joyful confusion about all questions of belief and a 'silly' play to enjoy on the way. And we must agree with Hippolyta, if imagination is to "amend" the inadequacy of the performance:

> *It must be your imagination then, and not theirs.*

That this is undoubtedly so, cannot be questioned. It is perhaps one of the striking definitions of theatre (as opposed, say, to film) : the actor's performance is not 'reality'. We just hope he will draw us so closely to the emotional truth that it feels real and our imagination has not too big a gap to jump.

Shakespeare - as commentator - tells us so directly. The Chorus introducing the play *Henry V* laments that if he is to show us the battle of Agincourt he lacks "vasty fields", horses, armies. Therefore:

> *....let us ...*
> *On your imaginary forces work.*
> *.........*
> *Piece out our imperfections with your thoughts:*
> *Into a thousand parts divide one man,*
> *And make imaginary puissance;*   puissance = military force
> *Think, when we talk of horses, that you see them*
> *Printing their proud hoofs i' th' receiving earth;*
> *For 'tis your thoughts that now must deck our kings,*
> *Carry them here and there.....*

> **Henry V   Chorus 17 ... 29**

It is our imagination that is needed to fill out the meagre staging of the action. But, of course, that is not the whole story. There is also the extraordinary and revealing part that the action – the art and the artifice - has in awakening our imagination.

This is the poet's job - the painter's capability, the musician's challenge, the dance-master's knack - to gift us glimpses of some other actuality that lives in the imagination. There is a magical fulfilment that marries the artist's imagination to the imagination of the viewer, the listener, the dreamer – the human mind.   What indeed would we be without this capability? Hamlet's answer to that is:

A beast. No more.

Hamlet   IV iv 35

6: Passion

> *Away to heaven, respective lenity,*
> *And fire-eyed fury be my conduct now.*
>
> **Romeo & Juliet III i 122 – 123**

> *Blow winds and crack your cheeks! Rage! Blow!*
>
> **King Lear III ii 1**

> *What passion hangs these weights upon my tongue?*
> *I cannot speak......*
>
> **As You Like It I ii 245 – 246**

The life lived by the people who inhabit Shakespeare's plays
is a life of **passion**. To rise in anger or to fall in love is the action
of a moment. Deep gloom and dancing joy are more commonly
met than balanced reasonableness.

> *I have tremor cordis on me: my heart dances.*
> *But not for joy – not joy......*
>
> **The Winter's Tale I ii 110 -111**

Passion drives action. Passion spurs or inhibits every shift of
mood. And passion – a passionate clinging to an innermost sense
of direction, purpose and inevitability – dominates character.
External events and the advice or persuasion of other people
seldom has much effect compared with this vigorous inner
dynamic.   It follows that our modern search for motive,
justification or psychological explanation of a person's actions is
not always appropriate when discussing Shakespeare's characters.
Rather we must expect to meet each of them in full flood,
passionately active, without troubling ourselves too much as to
'why' this person behaves this way.   That *is* how she is. *This* is the
man.

So it is that Desdemona, puzzling to find a motive for
Othello's violent behaviour, hearing Emilia's hope that it should

be "no jealous toy concerning you", cries out "I never gave him cause!" Which prompts Emilia to say:

> *But jealous souls will not be answer'd so;*
> *They are not ever jealous for the cause,*
> *But jealous for they are jealous.*

Othello III iv 163-165

It is not only the passionate expression of anger and love that Shakespeare gives us, but of every kind of desire, repulsion, lust, loyalty, self-promotion, patriotism, eagerness, care and kindness, destructiveness and despair.

Passion drives action – or, maybe, causes paralysis.

Orlando, the young hero of *As You Like It*, having shown us his anger and integrity in a confrontation with his wicked older brother (who kept him as a "peasant, obscuring and hiding from me all gentleman-like qualities" I i 65); and having shown us his manly, sporting courage and skill in his fight with Charles the Wrestler; this Orlando is now struck dumb when Rosalind - never at a loss for words, but also suddenly in love - speaks to him:

> *Sir, you have wrestled well and overthrown*
> *More than your enemies.*

As You Like It I ii 242 - 243

Unable to reply, paralysed by the surge of emotion within him, Orlando can only stare as she walks away. When he does find his voice it is to say:

> *What passion hangs these weights upon my tongue?*
> *I cannot speak to her – yet she hath urged conference.*
> *O poor Orlando, thou art overthrown!*
> *Or Charles - or something weaker - masters thee.*

As You Like It I ii 245 - 248

Such is the power of "this something weaker" when it lights the fire of passion in this man.

Fortunately for us, most of those who fall in love in the plays *are* able to speak and we gain a world of poetry from them.

The role of Passion – given a capital letter so that we might consider it almost as a person, a protagonist that drives the action - cannot be better illustrated than in the two great plays which begin with a single irrational, emotional outburst from the human protagonist - a King in each case - *The Winter's Tale* and *King Lear*.

These two take their places in the following pages, along with the three plays which retell the great, legendary love stories of European culture: *Romeo and Juliet*, *Antony and Cleopatra* and the extraordinary *Troilus and Cressida* which delves back to the very birth of literature, playing havoc with the reputations of the heroes of the Trojan war, while robbing them of their conversations with the Gods.

Love, Jealousy, Anger – Shakespeare's word is "Rage".

First then: *Romeo and Juliet.*

The passion which fuels the feud between the Capulets and Montagues is not a lesser passion than that displayed by the two lovers of the title. Within the Capulet family, cousin Tybalt and Juliet's father are equally matched in their emotional outbursts. Romeo's mother, Lady Montague, suffers such anguish at news of her son's banishment that it kills her. The intense activity of the townspeople in the final act of the play, after the deaths of the lovers, illustrates the passionate behaviour of the society. In the imagination of the English (then and now) this is how life in Italy is: driven by emotional excess.

All this could have been healed by the marriage. That is Friar Laurence's hope. He agrees to perform the ceremony....

> *For this alliance may so happy prove*
> *To turn your households' rancour to pure love.*
> **Romeo & Juliet II iii 91 – 92**

Romeo is determined to speak fair and act respectfully when he meets Tybalt in the street an hour or so after the marriage. But Mercutio's taunts and Tybalt's rapier put an end to that. Romeo's friend dies – and he is taken over by passionate rage.

72

Away to heaven, respective lenity,
And fire-eyed fury be my conduct now.

Romeo & Juliet III i 122 - 123

- - - - -

Aside: Even at this hectic dramatic moment our ears
might pick up a pleasing musical pun around the word
"conduct". Before Romeo arrives Tybalt refers to
Mercutio's friendship with Romeo and uses the word
"consort". To which Mercutio replies, "Consort?
What, dost thou make us minstrels?" Now, far from
the harmony which Romeo wishes to introduce, "fire-
eyed fury" is 'conducting' an orchestra of discord.

- - - - -

The tragic plot develops from this moment of anger followed
by action. It is even implied that Mercutio's death is due to
Romeo's action. "Why the devil came you between us?" says the
joking, dying Mercutio – suggesting that his fight with Tybalt was,
until Romeo interfered, a careful dance avoiding hurt.

We cannot, do not blame Romeo for his action. Honour,
manliness and just revenge spurs him on to attack Tybalt. And yet,
if only he had somehow kept cool and stayed with "the reason that
I have to love thee" [III i 60], ridden out the taunts, remembered
the marriage. No. He is responsible. He knows he is:

Oh, I am Fortune's fool.

Romeo & Juliet III i 135

It is doom. It is death. From this moment in Act III the
tragic events inevitably follow.

In *The Winter's Tale* such a moment occurs in Act I.

This is an extreme example of the irrational 'conduct' of
Passion creating a crisis which drives a Shakespearean plot.
Leontes, King of Sicily, switches suddenly out of his role as loving

father and respected diplomat (a brief Shakespearean portrait of a very good King) to become a jealous tyrant.

He has been watching his wife, Hermione, playfully persuading his best friend Polixenes that he should extend his visit to Sicily – not go home to his kingdom, Bohemia, where his family wait for him. Hermione is pregnant. She is due to give birth. Polixenes has been staying with them for nine months. Is it possible.... ? Of course it is utterly *im*possible that Polixenes could have seduced Hermione, practically the day he arrived, and be the father of this about-to-be-born child. But such is the dynamic power of the seed of jealousy which suddenly takes root in Leontes' heart that he is completely commanded by it, convinced and determined to act: driven by the overpowering belief that *this is* so.

This unchecked – indeed, uncheckable – drive of Passion, becomes a physical, bodily possession.

I have tremor cordis on me: my heart dances.
But not for joy – not joy......

The Winter's Tale I ii 110 -111

There do not seem to be any clues in the script as to *why* this conviction overwhelms Leontes in this way. Commentators and scholars have puzzled over the lack of motive for hundreds of years! We can only return to Emilia's comment: he is jealous because he is jealous.

The play, ***The Winter's Tale***, which grows from this moment, follows Shakespeare's oddest plot-line. Switching from Sicily to Bohemia, from deplorable tragedy to sunny rustic comedy, the story includes an abandoned baby, a disguised prince, a shipwreck, a pickpocket, life that returns from death, a visit to Apollo's shrine at Delphi and the marvellous stage direction, "Exit pursued by a bear". It is one of Shakespeare's last three plays, often labelled 'plays of reconciliation', and tells, among other things, of Leontes' desperate and painful journey to redeem the consequences of his (literally) fatal surrender to passion. The fantastic imagery of the play offers extraordinary material for the consideration of the folly and aspiration of human beings.

- - - - -

Aside. The pickpocket, named Autolycus [pronounced "Or–toll–akuss" with the emphasis on the "toll"], supplies a deal of humour in the second half of the play. His immoral, hurtful stealing and cheating (taking the market money from the naïve shepherd boy, selling worthless magical trinkets to the shepherdesses) is so neatly performed that we lose all sense of outrage. We are conned into complicit acceptance of his behaviour. Unlike Leontes he appears to act with cool cunning and to have no feelings other than glee at his own success and cleverness. He is incapable of repentance.

- - - - -

And so to *King Lear.*

When his youngest about-to-be-married daughter, Cordelia, is invited to join in the game played by her sisters - speaking of their love for their father as the most precious aspect of their lives - she cannot 'heave her heart into her mouth' but must subject her tongue to the censorship of truth-telling.

This inner integrity is not a welcome guest at this king's court. The emphasis is clearly stated by Lear when he demands to be told by his daughters "Which of you shall we say doth love us most?". The use of that royal "we" – repeated: "us" – demonstrates the hierarchical, political realm that his mind inhabits. Of course Cordelia 'should' have known this – and responded accordingly. But, alas, no. She is driven by a passion equal to, or even more fervent than the passion of erotic love – namely the passion for Truth.

- - - - -

Aside. But, of course, not 'Alas': if one aspiration shines above others for Shakespeare, it is the hope of inner Truth. All the love and tragedy, all the comedy, all the poetic glory and the inner working of each plot, point to the one truly heroic quest: the search for integrity and truth. This is Brutus, this is Hamlet, this is Rosalind and Desdemona and many others – many of them fated to be caught in the tragic spirals of a destructive society, but no less admirable for that.

- - - - -

CORDELIA.   *Good my lord,*
     You have begot me, bred me, lov'd me; I
     Return those duties back as are right fit,
     Obey you, love you, and most honour you.
     Why have my sisters husbands, if they say
     They love you all? Haply, when I shall wed,
     That lord whose hand must take my plight shall carry
     Half my love with him, half my care and duty.
     Sure I shall never marry like my sisters,
     To love my father all.

LEAR.   *But goes thy heart with this?*

CORDELIA. *Ay, good my lord.*

LEAR.   *So young, and so untender?*

CORDELIA. *So young, my lord, and true.*

LEAR.   *Let it be so! thy truth then be thy dower!*

King Lear I 94 – 107

And, swearing by astrological "operation", witchcraft and the pagan gods, he disinherits his most loved daughter, Cordelia - whose name does not take much stretching to become 'Coeur de Lear'. In banishing her he does indeed tear out his own heart.

And puts himself at the mercy of his other daughters. His original plan – the purpose of the gathering where the public statement of daughter-father love should be made – was to divide his kingdom in three and retire comfortably to live with Cordelia and her husband. Now he must look for lodging with one of the other daughters. Incensed by Goneril, the eldest, who has accused the knights who accompany him – whom he describes as "men of choice and rarest parts" - of being a "disordered rabble", Lear calls up this horrible curse upon her:

> *Hear, Nature, hear! Dear Goddess, hear!*
> *Suspend thy purpose, if thou didst intend*
> *To make this creature fruitful!*
> *Into her womb convey sterility!*
> *Dry up in her the organs of increase,*
> *And from her derogate body never spring*
> *A babe to honour her.*
>
> King Lear I iv 269 – 275

He wishes the "Goddess", Nature, to destroy the very gender attributes possessed by the woman: calling on the female to attack the female. Such curses are bound to rebound upon the man who dares such things, and it not long before this feminine fury has entered him:

> *Oh, how this mother swells up toward my heart*
> *Hysterica passio, down my climbing sorrow.*
>
> King Lear II iv 55 - 56

The strangeness – the physicality and complexity - of all this sweeps on through the play. Alongside the cruel actions of humankind that drive the plot, Nature herself appears to be taking part. Out on a wild heath, Lear staggers his way to madness, and calls upon the elements to bolster the angry chaos that he has promoted:

> *Blow winds and crack your cheeks! Rage! Blow!*
>
> King Lear III ii 1

So it is that human passion is echoed and enhanced by Nature.

Many tempests blow their way into Shakespeare's plays. Especially interesting are the sea storms that lead to shipwreck and the stranding of protagonists on strange, unknown coasts. Echoing, symbolising, becoming the very state of mind of the people in the play, it is difficult to define whether such storms are 'real' or indeed …

> *The tempest in my mind*
> **King Lear III iv 12**

Both Lear and Leontes are possessed by irrational, uncontrollable passion which drives their action. It is not that they have any reasonable, conscious choice in the matter - yet they bring upon themselves and their families devastating disaster.

Things are different in ***Antony and Cleopatra.***

They are the rulers of the known world: Cleopatra, Queen of Egypt, Antony one of the Triumvirate who command Rome's global Empire. But their passionate erotic relationship overrules all other considerations. Political reality is set aside. Rome stands for order, reason and control, but Antony decrees:

> *Let Rome in Tiber melt, and the wide arch*
> *Of the ranged empire fall. Here is my space.*
> *Kingdoms are clay: our dungy earth alike*
> *Feeds beast as man: the nobleness of life*
> *Is to do thus.*
> **Antony and Cleopatra I i 33 - 7**

"Here" in Egypt and in Cleopatra's arms is Antony's "space". To "do thus" - as the unnecessary stage direction written in by editors tells us – is to sexually embrace. We cannot escape the symbolism that is presented in this play: Rome is rationality and order – Egypt is voluptuousness and irresponsibility. Antony chooses the latter.

- - - - -

Aside. Note in passing the other images Antony gives us: "clay", "earth", "dung", "beast" all "feeding" – so much sensual, messy stuff claiming "nobleness" against the "arch" of "empire" and "kingdom". The stones of Rome will "melt"! - and be washed away in the river Tiber – if Antony has his way. Fluid sexuality replaces iron medallion as the badge of noblest humanity.

- - - - -

The cold political reality which challenges their choice is acted out by - or takes shape in – or, quite simply, in this play *is* - Octavius Caesar. It is he who has summoned Antony to Rome at the beginning of the play. It is he who, as the antagonism moves into war, manages battles by sea and land much better than Antony - and therefore wins.

At the end of the play, after Antony's death, we witness the meeting of Octavius and Cleopatra. A confrontation between two extremes of humanity: the hard, rational, dignified man faces the evasive, sensual woman. Control versus intuition. Order versus sexuality. As if the struggle between reasonableness and passion is that between male and female.

This idea occurs elsewhere in Shakespeare, especially in the sonnets.

- - - - -

Aside. For those who wish to claim that the sonnets speak of personal experience, every sort of seduction story has been read into this (and other) sonnet(s), giving Shakespeare, the man, a secret bi-sexual lifestyle suitably exotic to attract our attention. Even if this be so, nothing prevents the poet Shakespeare giving us a symbolic presentation.

- - - - -

Two loves I have of comfort and despair,
Which like two spirits do suggest me still:
The better angel is a man right fair,
The worser spirit a woman coloured ill.
To win me soon to hell my female evil
Tempteth my better angel from my side,
And would corrupt my saint to be a devil,
Wooing his purity with her foul pride.
And whether that my angel be turned fiend,
Suspect I may, yet not directly tell,
But being both from me both to each friend,
I guess one angel in another's hell.
   Yet this shall I ne'er know, but live in doubt,
   Till my bad angel fire my good one out.

Sonnet 144

This is the internal, emotional struggle where the sensual-sexual diverts the rational mind away from 'good' intent. In the civilised world of reputation and social responsibility, a moral judgement is made: the diverting aspect becomes "my female evil" who opposes "the better angel" who "is a man right fair".

- - - - -

Aside. In the figures of classical myth, this is the struggle between Dionysus and Apollo. Apollonian characteristics are order and dignity, intellectual clarity: think of the cool beauty of Greek Sculpture. Dionysus is energetic and uncontrollable, fluid voluptuousness – belonging to an erotic dream world. It is lawfully reputable to behave with Apollonian good sense, but the lure of the murky lust of Dionysus may be irresistible.

- - - - -

In *Troilus and Cressida* the story of Homer's *Iliad* – and the further stories and legends that have attached themselves to it in the course of time - is turned into a seditious, salacious plot questioning honour and integrity, revelling in:

*Lechery, lechery, still wars and lechery! Nothing
else holds fashion.*
Troilus & Cressida V iii 193

Troilus, Hector and Paris are three of the Princes of Troy,
sons of King Priam. It was Paris who, when on a diplomatic visit
to Greece, started the conflict by seducing and abducting Helen,
wife of King Menelaus who now with his brother King
Agamemnon and the great warrior Achilles and all the vast Greek
and allied armies are besieging Troy.

Inside the city they live well. Daily dangerous forays are
made, but the warriors return to wives and children – or in the case
of Paris, who frequently stays out of the battle ("I would fain have
armed today, but my Nell would not have it so"), to Helen:

> *The mortal Venus, the heart-blood of beauty,
> love's visible soul...*
> **Troilus & Cressida III i 30**

Words spoken for us: history, legend, poetry, everybody's
fantastic expectation... but, here, by a servant who cannot really
know her. When she appears a few moments later she is shallow
and demanding - seductive but of little wit.

Nevertheless Helen is the allegorical centre. Troy is a
society defending Beauty. What better place could be found for
the wooing of virgin Cressida by the gallant Troilus whose name
means Truth?

Outside the walls, camped on the plain by the sea, are the
quarrelsome, boasting, unimaginative Greeks. Their socio-
political philosophy is famously described by Ulysses, the cleverest
of the commanders, whose speech of more than 130 lines [I iii 54 –
184 +] is often quoted to show that Shakespeare 'believed in' order,
civil stability and political restraint.

But that is only half the picture – Troy is the other half.
Even then any expectation that the people on either side will live
up to their ideals must be abandoned in this play: Ulysses himself,
within moments of declaring the proper hierarchical 'order' of the
Greek chain of command, is plotting to deceive, embarrass and
undermine Achilles, their greatest soldier. And within Troy –

81

especially in the seduction of, and the subsequent behaviour of Cressida – integrity, trust, and hope succumb to war and lechery.

War and Lechery. Both born of Passion. If we must claim to know Shakespeare's 'beliefs' surely this is one: war and lechery lead to deceit, emotional and physical violence, despair and grief.

- - - - -

> **Aside.** The complexity of argument, the jokes and jibes – mostly of a blatantly sexual nature - make this an extremely difficult play to 'interpret'. Every aspect is turned on its head – even the horror of war is matched against bravery and honourable talk. It is thought that the only contemporary performance was privately for lawyers at the Inns of Court: intellectual entanglement was welcome there. To match the strangeness of the play, even the date of composition is disputed. It could be before *Hamlet* [1599] – certainly Troy was in his mind: Hamlet chooses as his inspiration for the actors, a speech about the death of Priam. But it might be much later, about the time it was first printed [1609], after *Lear* and *Antony and Cleopatra*. When the Folio was printed [1623] it nearly got left out, and was finally slipped into the already printed sequence with unnumbered pages between the *HISTORIES* and *TRAGEDIES*: it is not mentioned in the list of contents.

- - - - -

One noble character stands out: Hector – a candidate to be Shakespeare's bravest, most intelligent soldier. He is in favour of wide-awake reasonableness: human, diplomatic, commonsense. He wants to avoid blood-letting. He wants to end the war. In open council – a truly democratic debate among the princes – he contributes sanity:

> *Let Helen go!*
>> **Troilus and Cressida II ii 17**

But the other brothers rally to Paris's side: in particular young Troilus argues the value and validity of keeping Helen. Hector challenges them:

> *The reasons you allege do more conduce*
> *To the hot passion of distemp'red blood*
> *Than to make up a free determination*
> *'Twixt right and wrong; for pleasure and revenge*
> *Have ears more deaf than adders to the voice*
> *Of any true decision.*

Troilus and Cressida II ii 169 - 174

Here is the commonsensical, logical response to 'passion'. Hector's image of the deaf ears of Pleasure and Revenge allowing those addicted to bypass thoughts of restraint, conveniently summons up an adder as an example of deafness: linking us back to the snake in the garden of Eden who first persuaded Adam and Eve to disobey God.

It is powerfully appropriate that this argument - challenging the rule of passion - is presented by an honest warrior, rather than by a priest or a philosopher.

But we are not to be governed by good sense. This is war. And sexual conquest. Within moments Hector backs away:

> *Yet ne'ertheless,*
> *My spritely brethren, I propend to you*
> *In resolution to keep Helen still –*
> *For 'tis a cause that hath no mean dependence*
> *Upon our joint and several dignities.*

Troilus and Cressida II ii 190 - 194

Such is the power, even over Hector, of the concept of honour, and the loyalty he feels with his royal brothers. "Our joint and several dignities" concern pride and not losing face. Such is the rule of passion. Such is the tragedy.

Shakespeare is in no doubt: unbridled passion of the sort displayed in *Troilus and Cressida* becomes the subject of one of his sonnets.

> The expense of spirit in a waste of shame
> Is lust in action; and till action, lust
> Is perjur'd, murd'rous, bloody, full of blame,
> Savage, extreme, rude, cruel, not to trust;
> Enjoy'd no sooner but despised straight;
> Past reason hunted, and, no sooner had,
> Past reason hated, as a swallow'd bait,
> On purpose laid to make the taker mad –
> Mad in pursuit, and in possession so;
> Had, having, and in quest to have, extreme;
> A bliss in proof, and prov'd, a very woe;
> Before a joy proposed, behind a dream.
> > All this the world well knows; yet none knows well
> > To shun the heaven that leads men to this hell.

Sonnet 129

These thoughts may be taken as a rebuke to those who wish to go to war, and those who seek power, just as truly as the more obvious application to sexual desire. The bringing of the two together is not only the theme of the Trojan War – the 'rape' of Helen being the cause of it – but it is also Hamlet's perception of his uncle's crime.

Claudius murdered his bother so that he could have his brother's wife *and* could be king.

> Remorseless, treacherous, lecherous, kindless villain.

..is Hamlet's passionate description of this man. Yet even in the uttering of these words he realises that he is allowing his anger to distort his judgement – he is in danger of becoming "Passion's slave" and quickly rebukes himself:

> Why, what an ass am I! ..... About, my brains.

Hamlet II ii 578, 580,586

He calls upon his intelligence to balance himself.

We will be returning to the long soliloquy from which these lines are taken, in the next chapter. Hamlet is a great thinker – a debater with himself. It is one of the peculiarities which make the play so interesting: the four great solo speeches where he explores ideas and feelings – because Hamlet's inner world troubles and intrigues him. His compulsion is to see through all the 'seemings' that cover up the truth, as in the very first words we hear him speak, in reply to his mother's question about his grief for his father:

Why seems it so particular with thee?

This is his reply:

> *Seems, madam, Nay, it is. I know not 'seems.'*
> *'Tis not alone my inky cloak, good mother,*
> *Nor customary suits of solemn black,*
> *Nor windy suspiration of forc'd breath,*
> *No, nor the fruitful river in the eye,*
> *Nor the dejected havior of the visage,*
> *Together with all forms, moods, shapes of grief,*
> *That can denote me truly. These indeed seem,*
> *For they are actions that a man might play;*
> *But I have that within which passeth show -*
> *These but the trappings and the suits of woe.*

havior = behaviour
visage = face

Hamlet I ii 75 - 86

It is exactly "that within which passeth [= surpasses] show [= outward appearance]" that he is constantly exploring – matching thought with feeling. He is not helped by his decision "To put an antic disposition on" [I v 172] – that is: to appear to be mad – since the acting out of this 'disposition' comes close to pushing him over the edge into – if not actual madness – unbearable emotional stress.

Hamlet needs some help, some human warmth, to survive all that he meets outwardly - and invites inwardly. Fortunately his

85

friend Horatio is at hand, to whom he says in a small oasis of calm in the middle of the play:

> Dost thou hear?
> Since my dear soul was mistress of her choice,
> And could of men distinguish - her election
> Hath sealed thee for herself. For thou hast been
> As one, in suff'ring all, that suffers nothing,
> A man that Fortune's buffets and rewards
> Hast ta'en with equal thanks; and blest are those
> Whose blood and judgment are so well co-mingled
> That they are not a pipe for Fortune's finger
> To sound what stop she please. Give me that man
> That is not passion's slave, and I will wear him
> In my heart's core, ay, in my heart of heart,
> As I do thee.

seal – a legal stamp

ta'en = taken

pipe = flute / recorder

Hamlet III ii 62 – 74

The proximity of this speech of friendship to the passage where he gives advice to the actors who have visited Elsinore may not be entirely coincidence.

It is time to pay attention to that speech.

———

Hamlet's Speech to the Players

Act III scene ii   lines 1 – 40

As reproduced on the next two pages, this speech is laid out as in the Folio – as near as is readable and reasonable.

The punctuation and Capital letters are as in the Folio printing, as also the spread of words on each line.

But some spellings have been altered - such as leaving out the final "e" on 'smoothnesse' and 'winde'; writing 'Air' for 'Ayre', and "o'er" (= over) for 'ore' or "o're"; etc.

It is logical, earnest and energetic. A clear expression of Hamlet's - and Shakespeare's – belief in the role of Theatre.

We might pause to wonder why it should be here in the middle of the play *Hamlet*: nothing would be lost in terms of plot or drama if it were not here.

It's presence suggests, therefore, that this moment in Shakespeare's career was of special significance, and the whole of this play carries eloquent comment on his perception of Life and Art.

Are the seeds of *Lear* and *Othello* already germinating in his mind? Is the play-within-the-play an extra special ingredient that he delights in? How would he feel about some of the Clowns and Directors of modern theatre who "speak … more than is set down for them"?

Enter Hamlet, and two or three of the Players

HAM. Speak the Speech I pray you, as I pronounc'd it to you trippingly on the Tongue: But if you mouth it, as many of your Players do, I had as live the Town-Cryer had spoke my Lines: Nor do not saw the Air too much your hand thus, but use all gently ; for in the very Torrent, Tempest, and (as I may say) the Whirle-wind of Passion, you must acquire and beget a Temperance that may give it Smoothness. O it offends me to the Soul, to see a robustious Pery-wig-pated Fellow, tear a Passion to tatters, to very rags, to split the ears of the Groundlings: who (for the most part) are capable of nothing, but inexplicable dumb shows, & noise: I could have such a Fellow whipt for o'erdoing Termagant: it out-Herod's Herod. Pray you avoid it.

PLAYER. I warrant your Honour.

HAM. Be not too tame neither; but let your own Discretion be your Tutor. Suit the Action to the Word, the Word to the Action, with this special observance: That you o'erstop not the modesty of Nature; for any thing so over-done, is from the purpose of Playing, whose end both at the first and now,was and is,to hold, as 'twere the Mirror up to Nature; to show Virtue her own Feature, Scorn her own Image, and the very Age and

88

Body of the Time, his form and pressure.   Now, this over-done, or come tardy off, though it make the unskil-full laugh, cannot but make the Judicious grieve; The censure of the which One, must in your allowance o'erweigh a whole Theatre of Others. Oh, there be Players that I have seen Play, and heard others praise, and that highly (not to speak it profanely) that neither having the accent of Christians, nor the gait of Christian, Pagan, or Norman, have so strutted and bellowed, that I have thought some of Nature's Journey-men had made men, and not made them well, they imitated Humanity so ab-ominably.

PLAY. I hope we have reform'd that indifferently with us, Sir.

HAM. O reform it altogether.   And let those that play your Clowns, speak no more than is set down for them.   For there be of them, that will themselves laugh, to set on some quantity of barren Spectators to laugh too,   though in the mean time, some necessary Question of the Play be then to be considered: that's villainous, & shows a most pitiful Ambition in the Fool that uses it. Go make you ready.

Exit Players.

Enter Polonius, Rosincrance, and Guildenstarene.

7. Advice on Acting

...o'erstop not the modesty of Nature...

Hamlet III ii 18

The arrival of the players at Elsinore is a pivotal moment in *Hamlet*. When he meets them, Hamlet immediately resorts to 'acting' himself, starting to declaim the speech – which is then picked up by the first player – about Pyrrhus and the death of King Priam: an excessively rhetorical, over-the-top, melodramatic piece (which may be a parody of a current play about the Trojan War already in the repertoire of the Chamberlain's Men).

Immediately after this he asks Polonius to

... see the players well bestowed....

...commenting that they are

....the abstract and brief chroniclers of the time.

Hamlet II ii 522

... and should therefore "be well used". As they leave he announces "we'll hear a play tomorrow" and, drawing aside the first player, asks him whether his company can play *The Murder of Gonzago* and insert into it "a dozen or sixteen lines which I would set down".   This is agreed, and, left alone, Hamlet launches into the second of his four great soliloquies.

In this self-critical, passionate, complicated speech he marvels at the emotional performance of the first player, who, retelling the death of Priam, had tears in his eyes, a broken voice and "his whole function suiting with the forms to his conceit".

And all for nothing.
For Hecuba?
What's Hecuba to him or he to Hecuba
That he should weep for her?

Hamlet II ii 555 - 557

Hecuba is Priam's wife. The whole thing is a fiction, a legend, an old tale – a poem proclaimed.

> *Yet I*
> *A dull and muddy-mettled rascal...*
>
> *... can say nothing, no, not for a king*
> *Upon whose property and most dear life*
> *A damned defeat was made.*

Hamlet II ii 563 ... 568

So the actor has shown enormous passion over the *fictitious* events – but Hamlet cannot bring himself to act, or speak or show real emotion for the *actual* murder of his father which calls for exposure and revenge.

- - - - -

Aside. In the course of the speech he does achieve an emotional peak in himself [as quoted in the previous chapter], but then condemns himself because this has not led to action. This relationship between feeling, thought and *action* is one of the major themes of the play and the prime subject of the most famous soliloquy: "To be or not to be".

- - - - -

Somewhere in his mind he finds the thought that before taking revenge he ought to hesitate because the ghost who revealed the alleged murder to him might be an evil spirit. This is, at present, the only 'evidence' of the murder that he has. He should have 'proof' before taking action. Therefore the instruction to the players to perform the following evening a play which has in it a scene resembling that murder in the garden that the ghost told him about. For "guilty creatures sitting at a play" will reveal themselves.

> *The play's the thing*
> *Wherein I'll catch the conscience of the King.*

Hamlet II ii 603

91

It is as the actors gather to present this play that he meets them and gives them the lecture on how to act.

- - - - -

Aside. One of the delights of theatre is to spot moments when an actor is not quite acting. So, in delivering this homily on acting, an actor playing the part of a Prince gives instructions to 'actors' – played by actors - on how to act! Add to this that the author of this speech was himself an actor. Is Shakespeare then using Hamlet as a mouthpiece to give his fellow actors a lesson?

- - - - -

In the version of the speech, printed on pages 88-89, with punctuation and capital letters as they appear in the Folio text, there are a few unfamiliar readings. So we have the word "o'erstop" rather than the word generally printed today: "o'erstep". [In each case "o'er" is the word "over" shortened.] This seems a good reading: to 'overstop' is presumably a musical allusion, meaning perhaps to pitch too high or blow too hard. That's what we must not do to Nature: not abuse her, but treat her 'modestly'.

We note, however, some inconsistency here. It was exactly that 'overtopping' (overstopping/overstepping) in the actor's telling of the death of Priam – the passion, the tears in his eyes - which Hamlet found so effective. The subject was violent death - the death of husband or father – the stunning effect upon Hecuba of witnessing this. There was, in the actor's performance, a remarkable display of 'true' feeling: a display which Hamlet was unable to match in a 'real' situation.

This leads to the discussion concerning how much 'passion' an actor should show, and is the subject of the first part of Hamlet's speech instructing the players. On the one hand the actor is expected to be in...

.. the very Torrent, Tempest, and... Whirle-wind of... Passion..

92

But on the other he must somehow ...

...acquire and beget a Temperance that may give it Smoothness.

Maybe - if the script is good enough – there is enough Passion there, already, in the writing, so there is no need to add more torrents of emotion. Do not "overdo Termagant" or "out-Herod Herod".

- - - - -

Aside. In medieval plays the degree of rant was a measure of villainy. The frequently appearing characters of Termagant (a turbaned, pagan spirit) and King Herod (responsible for the mass slaughter of children – "the innocents") were the ultimate ranters. When Falstaff feigns death in the battle of Shrewsbury he says:

'Sblood, 'twas time to counterfeit, or that hot Termagant Scot had paid me scot and lot too.

Henry IV Part 1   V iv 111

The Termagant Scot is the rebel Douglas.

- - - - -

It is then, in the second part of the speech, that Hamlet exhorts the players to "be not too tame neither...", to use their Discretion, to match Word and Action. It is here that he exhorts them to "..o'erstop not the modesty of Nature"

Clearly he is struggling with the dilemma: how much passion 'should' the actor display. And – while on the one hand we want to "be natural" – yet we are attempting to accomplish that "end" and "purpose" of "playing" which is:

To hold, as 'twere the Mirror up to Nature.

And this Nature – the same and yet not the same as that which portrays the every day emotion (and passion) – is a complex thing involving Virtue's "Feature", Scorn's "Image" and the very form and pressure of the "Age and Body of the Time".

93

It would be wise to ponder this a little deeper: and the prompt to do this lies in that little phrase in the middle of the line:

...to hold, as 'twere the Mirror up to Nature...

Notice there is no comma before the word 'Mirror'. The "as 'twere" attaches to - and questions the significance of – the word "mirror", not the act of holding. So he is talking about the theatre "as if it were a mirror" – suggesting that this is a new thought, a struggling-to-get-hold-of meaning.

It might be worth noting that there is someone else who uses that phrase "as it were" in the play. When Claudius, on his very first appearance is justifying his hasty marriage, so soon after the funeral of Hamlet's father (his new wife's former husband), he says that it is:

....as 'twere with a defeated joy,
With one auspicious, and one dropping eye,
With mirth in funeral, and with dirge in marriage...
Hamlet I ii 10 - 12

.. that he has taken her "to wife". By putting these opposite aspects alongside each other, Claudius is trying to prove that he is neither avoiding the truth nor neglecting to move on.

There is a shift of precision – a softening of clarity – in this "as 'twere". Claudius is a politician. Hamlet is a seeker after truth. Both resort to a figure of speech which suggests that plain speaking is not quite as simple as we would wish.

94

8: Looking in the Mirror

> *O that I were a mockery king of snow,*
> *Standing before the sun of Bolingbroke*
> *To melt myself away in water drops!*
> *Good king, great king, and yet not greatly good,*
> *An if my word be sterling yet in England,*
> *Let it command a mirror hither straight,*
> *That it may show me what a face I have*
> *Since it is bankrupt of his majesty.*

Richard II   IV   i   259 - 266

Surprisingly the word 'mirror' occurs only a dozen times in the whole of Shakespeare's work: the word 'glass' (meaning a looking-glass or mirror) slightly more often. There are four - two mirrors, two glasses - in ***Hamlet***. Most of the mirrors and glasses reflect a simple aspect, such as Ophelia's lament that the seeming-mad Prince Hamlet was once a proper courtier:

> *The glass of fashion and the mould of form.*

Hamlet   III   i   154

So, in the history plays the Duke of Salisbury, hit by a cannon ball, dying on stage, is described by brave Talbot as the...

> *... mirror of all martial men.*

And the former King Henry IV is praised because his...

> *... wisdom was a mirror to the wisest.*

Both quotations from the Henry VI plays

King Henry V, in the Act II Prologue of ***Henry V***, is described as....

> *... a mirror of all Christian Kings.*

95

Alongside – and after – these simple 'mirror' images comes the encounter looked at in Chapter 6 [page 64] when the un-kinged Richard II asks for a mirror. Before the dramatic gesture of breaking the mirror, Richard looks into it and sees.... himself.

> *Give me that glass, and therein will I read.*
> *No deeper wrinkles yet? Hath sorrow struck*
> *So many blows upon this face of mine*
> *And made no deeper wounds? O flatt'ring glass,*
> *Like to my followers in prosperity,*
> *Thou dost beguile me!*
>
> **Richard II   IV i 275 - 280**

"No deeper wrinkles yet". His face does not show – or rather the mirror does not show – the truth. He appears unchanged from the days when he had power. The mirror has joined the conspiracy which denies his pain: it shows him still a king of glory.

But that, of course, would be the theological, traditional, God-given Truth – not the mundane aspects of worldly political manoeuvring, but the eternal reality: because no-one has the right to dethrone God's anointed monarch, and he is therefore 'truly' still a King – and the "glory shineth in this face" **[line 287]**. If this is the case, then the mirror – far from dishonest flattery – reveals the true Nature: things as they really are.

It cannot be over-emphasised how significant this dethronement of Richard is as a moment of history. It is referred to (and lamented) several times in Shakespeare's 'History' plays. Henry V before the battle of Agincourt prays that God will be on his side and:

> *Not to-day, O Lord*
> *O not today, think not upon the fault*
> *My father made in compassing the crown*
>
> **Henry V   IV i 289-290**

It was a hot political issue, food for potential rebels. The three plays, chronicling the battles between the Houses of York and

Lancaster, disputing who would be "truly" King, were written several years before *Richard II* . [See list of plays: page 117] There is a moment when Richard (later Duke of York: father to the infamous Richard III) asks the dying Mortimer to explain "what cause that was" which had ruled his life's struggles. He gets a lengthy history lesson!

> *Henry the Fourth, grandfather to this king* [2]
> *Deposed his nephew* [3] *Richard, Edward's son,*
> *The first begotten and the lawful heir*
> *Of Edward, king, the third* [4] *of that descent,*
> *During whose reign......*
>
> **Henry VI pt 1   II   v   63 - 67**

The scene of this un-kinging is, therefore, one of the central moment's of English history which all of Shakespeare's audience would appreciate.

The lengthy enactment of the calling for and looking into the mirror carries more weight, therefore, than we might at first suppose.   This is a significant mirror which might be linked to mirrors in fairy tales and myth which reveal secrets – or truths.

Looking in a mirror in order to see oneself may be a surprising act: or a challenge.

In *Julius Caesar* Cassius challenges Brutus to acknowledge his true, hidden, passionate disturbance, and uses the metaphor of a mirror to achieve this. *Julius Caesar* is one of the plays written between 1596 and 1600 – that is after *Richard II* and before *Hamlet* – and it could well be that the image of the mirror as truth-teller has grown in Shakespeare's mind.

---

[2] King Henry VI

[3] Actually his cousin – words of family relationships can get confusing: so "cousin" is sometimes used for nephew, uncle etc.

[4] Edward III father to Edward the Black Prince (Richard II's father) and John of Gaunt (Bolingbroke/Henry IV's father).

Brutus dismisses his awkward behaviour and his neglect of his friends as no worse…

> *Than that poor Brutus with himself at war*
> *Forgets the shows of love to other men.*

Which prompts the following exchange:

CASSIUS. *Then, Brutus, I have much mistook your passion,*
By means whereof this breast of mine hath buried
Thoughts of great value, worthy cogitations.
Tell me, good Brutus, can you see your face?

BRUTUS. *No, Cassius, for the eye sees not itself*
But by reflection, by some other things.

CASSIUS. *'Tis just,*
And it is very much lamented, Brutus,
That you have no such mirrors, as will turn
Your hidden worthiness into your eye,
That you might see your shadow.
I have heard,
Where many of the best respect in Rome,
(Except immortal Caesar) speaking of Brutus,
And groaning underneath this age's yoke,
Have wish'd, that noble Brutus had his eyes.

BRUTUS. *Into what dangers would you lead me, Cassius,*
That you would have me seek into myself
For that which is not in me?

CASSIUS. *Therefore, good Brutus, be prepared to hear,*
And since you know you cannot see yourself
So well as by reflection, I your glass
Will modestly discover to yourself
That of yourself which you yet know not of.

Julius Caesar I ii 46 - 70

Note the return of the word "shadow". This is the reflection and the unseen portrait of himself: namely the dark part of Brutus's unconscious where is hidden the passionate belief that there is no way to stop Julius Caesar proclaiming himself a King (or a God), except by killing him. Such is Brutus's Apollonian purity – his integrity, his honour, his rational control of himself – that he cannot conceive of himself taking part in such a dreadful action. Gradually, following Cassius's prompting, he is able to hear the voice inside himself and debate the possibility. We hear him do it some time later when he is alone on stage in a speech - the first Shakespearean 'soliloquy' of the Hamlet kind - which begins:

It must be by his death...
Julius Caesar II i 10

The mirror which Cassius becomes is therefore the mirror which shows Brutus what he wishes to deny. It is the magic mirror which reveals Truth.

This, then, is perhaps "the purpose of playing": to hold up a mirror which promotes new consciousness – which confronts us with a truth not seen before.

Following Hamlet's lecture is the scene in which the players perform the play. The lecture was in prose. So are the exchanges between Hamlet and the King, the Queen, Ophelia, Polonius, *and* Rosencrantz and Guildenstern – a complete line up of all the characters with whom Hamlet is at odds – as they gather to watch the play. But the busy prose-action of all this is for a long quiet moment pushed aside by those 40 lines of verse which are Hamlet's thoughts on friendship and the instant drama, shared with Horatio [see page 86]. If anyone is looking for the soul of Hamlet - his deepest care and purpose – here it is, at the very centre of the play *Hamlet* just preceding the drama of the drama.

The play is performed. Claudius, deeply disturbed, leaves his seat and calls for lights and rushes from the room. Forcing himself to his knees in the chapel, he debates with his conscience.

Seeing the enactment of his murder portrayed on the stage, he can no longer deny it. It was there – in front of him. His conscious mind is forced to grapple with it. Earlier he has admitted in an aside that he has a "heavy burden" which has been 'sugared over' by "devotion's image and pious action" [III i 45 – 55], but the actual acknowledgement of the deed, he has not allowed until now. Now he uses the words "a brother's murder".

- - - - -

Aside. Cleverly, this is the moment when we in the audience also know for certain that he did the murder. Though it was a convincing performance, we had no more certainty than Hamlet that the ghost was telling the truth.

- - - - -

> *O, my offence is rank, it smells to heaven;*
> *It hath the primal eldest curse upon't,* [= upon it]
> *A brother's murder!*

Even so is there not such a thing as prayer – and forgiveness…

> *What if this cursed hand*
> *Were thicker than itself with brother's blood,*
> *Is there not rain enough in the sweet heavens*
> *To wash it white as snow?*

And after all:

> *My fault is past.*

But all the past now confronts him and the debate in his mind becomes the debate which must concern us all. Is there, beyond the concerns of the mundane worldly ambition, some True Value against which should be measured the worth of our actions? The Crown, the Queen – he knows only too well that …

> *In the corrupted currents of this world*
> *Offence's gilded hand may shove by justice,*
> ['wicked' is an adjective, *And oft 'tis seen the wicked prize itself*
> 'prize' a noun] *Buys out the law….*

But that is not the point, for Claudius is struggling with his soul and the arguments about 'heaven', and so…

> *... it is not so above.*
> *There is no shuffling; there the action lies*
> *In his true nature...*

Hamlet III iii 36 62

[Emphasis on the twice spoken "there"; "his" is the action's.]

So the mirror of the play has brought Claudius to consider the place – "above" - where True Nature cannot be avoided. And this is divine truth: ultimate, spiritual soul-truth.

Hamlet, much excited by the events at the play, is on his way to visit his mother in her bedroom and comes across Claudius kneeling as if in prayer. "Now might I do it": now he might kill him. But, if Claudius is praying, his soul will go to heaven: and this gives Hamlet the excuse not to kill him.

- - - - -

Aside. Back in Act II scene ii lines 573-6 [see pages 84 & 91] Hamlet accused himself of being "pigeon-livered" for failing to kill Claudius. He feels he 'should' do it. It is a command of the ghost, his father. But he wanted to test the ghost's truth (he has done so with the play) and now he has another 'excuse' for not doing it. Why this hesitation? Are those who accuse him of 'not being able to make up his mind' and 'failing' to act, correct? Or is there a much deeper curb that controls him: namely the knowledge that murder is wrong and that he, Hamlet, is a seeker of integrity, a free thinking Renaissance man – free, that is, from the chains of revenge, religion, tradition, and hierarchical politics. He *thinks* that he should be more like Fortinbras: but his actions are driven by a deep, undivulged, *knowing* that he has a higher calling.

- - - - -

101

So he carries on to his mother's room, in his state of high excitement, wishing to confront her with the situation. Here it is that Hamlet proposes to "hold the mirror" up for her.

> *Come, come, and sit you down. You shall not budge.*
> *You go not till I set you up a glass*
> *Where you may see the inmost part of you.*

Hamlet III iv 19-21

So alarmed is she by his behaviour (and this proposal?) that she cries out in fear, prompting Polonius who is spying on them, hidden "behind the arras" [III iii 28] to shout and struggle to get out, with the result that Hamlet's rapier.... The body of the dead Polonius remains on stage throughout the rest of the conversation between mother and son.

- - - - -

Aside. So having *not* killed Claudius, he has now killed Polonius. He asks "Is it the King?" [III iv 27] – but this is an after-thought: the killing was an instinctive action bred of the highly charged emotion of the moment, rather than a hoped for fulfilment of the delayed killing of Claudius.   Such is the momentum of the confrontation with his mother that this killing has to be pushed into the background, but it is an enormous act - a turning point of the play – and of Hamlet's life.

- - - - -

The glass which he sets up is a portrait of his father. Or rather two portraits [are they miniatures he had in is pocket, or are they pictures on the wall of Gertrude's room?] so that he compares his father's image and that of Claudius. With these 'shadows' - these 'mirrors' - he confronts his mother.

> *Look here upon this picture, and on this,*
> *The counterfeit presentment of two brothers.*
> *See what a grace was seated on this brow,*

Hyperion's curls, the front of Jove himself;
An eye like Mars....
       .... This was your husband.
Look you now what follows.
Here is your husband, like a mildew'd ear
Blasting his wholesome brother....

Hamlet III iv 54 ... 66

And his mirror fufills its task:

O Hamlet, speak no more.
Thou turnest mine eyes into my very soul...

Hamlet III iv 90

The as-it-were-mirror is not 'a play' but a couple of pictures held up by Hamlet, and the occasion is a very private one. But if the event "turnest mine eyes into my very soul" then it certainly has the same effect as the 'playing' had upon Claudius. And Gertrud's response reinforces – clarifies (if it needs to be clarified) - all that is implied in the mirroring-of-Nature image. She also is confronted by her soul-truth.

———————

There remains one more image. An image which is instantly recognised in a world that may know nothing of the plot of *Hamlet* - but knows that the man holding and talking to a skull is Hamlet.

If ever there was a mirror into which we might gaze with fascinated unease surely this is it: the Mirror of Death. If this were a medieval Mystery play Hamlet might meet a character named "Death". But here he is actually addressing his childhood friend, now dead: for this is the scene [V i - the graveyard scene] where among much else, comes the exact statement of Hamlet's age. He is, by the gravedigger's calendar, thirty years old. If then – as the gravedigger also tells us - this skull "hath lain in the earth three and twenty years", Hamlet was seven years old when Yorick, his father's jester, died.

103

The whole speech is possessed by sadness – the childhood loss of a friend, the inevitable arrival of death for each of us – but at the same time it is coupled with the recognisable riot of "flashes of merriment" which sparkle in so many of Shakespeare's plays, and to it is added a fresh image of that very "lady's chamber" where Hamlet's mother grappled with her soul.

> *Alas, poor Yorick! I knew him, Horatio. A fellow of infinite jest, of most excellent fancy. He hath borne me on his back a thousand times. And now how abhorred my imagination is, my gorge rises at it. Here hung those lips that I have kiss'd I know not how oft. Where be your gibes now? Your gambols? Your songs? Your flashes of merriment that were wont to set the table on a roar? No one now, to mock your own jeering? Quite chapfall'n? Now get you to my lady's chamber, and tell her, let her paint an inch thick, to this favour she must come. Make her laugh at that.*
>
> **Hamlet V i 180 - 190**

9: Beauty and Truth

Can I go forward when my heart is here?
Turn back dull earth and find thy centre out.

Romeo and Juliet II i 1 - 2

OPHELIA.   *My lord, I have remembrances of yours*
That I have longed long to re-deliver.
I pray you, now receive them.

HAMLET.   *No, no, I never gave you aught.*

OPHELIA.   *My honour'd lord, I know right well you did,*
And with them words of so sweet breath compos'd
As made the things more rich - then perfume left.
Take these again, for to the noble mind
Rich gifts wax poor when givers prove unkind.
There, my lord.

HAMLET.   *Ha, ha! Are you honest?*

OPHELIA.   *My lord?*

HAMLET.   *Are you fair?*

OPHELIA.   *What means your lordship?*

HAMLET.   *That if you be honest and fair, your Honesty*
should admit no discourse to your Beauty.

OPHELIA.   *Could Beauty, my lord, have better commerce than*
with Honesty?

Hamlet III i 93 - 110

No, indeed. In Art and in Life what better companions
than Beauty and Honesty? But Hamlet is in no mood to admit
that these, the ultimate worthy goals of action and intent, can

triumph over political and sexual corruption. To expose and make a just response to the murder of this father is his overwhelming task. So his reply is a cynical response to the complexity of the interwoven issues of the moment, one of which is Ophelia's rejection – dressed up as a response to his rejection of her.

- - - - -

> **Aside.** The 'truth' about did he/did he not really love Ophelia [one of the questions of the back-story of *Hamlet*] becomes the subject of their conversation a few lines later. Actors, directors and film-makers must grapple with this – readers and watchers of the play may, if they wish, avoid it. Every possibility from remote adoration to complete sexual intimacy is possible. In addition to the "words of so sweet breath" quoted here, there is, in the play, the letter which Polonius reads out, claiming it was written by Hamlet to Ophelia, and Ophelia's mad song [IV v 64] which includes the words "before you tumbled me".

- - - - -

If only he had the simple choice that Romeo has! Not that the 'simplicity' makes the enormity of Romeo's action any less courageous: hearing the joking insults yelled in the street by his friends, as he hides by the wall of the Capulet's garden, he is tempted to return to – to carry on with – his former life, but:

Can I go forward when my heart is here?

Not if he obeys the instructions that passion and reality give him:

Turn back dull earth and find thy centre out.

Romeo's Truth is revealed by Beauty. His action of love clarifies the lesson which the world of Verona needs to learn. Trapped in the "dull", "earthly" concerns of pride and hate, vitalised by the "rage" of the feuding families, nobody can escape or even understand that they need to escape. The young men about town thrive on their bawdy banter - utterly at odds with the direct and delightful exchanges between Romeo and Juliet which portray a 'true' human warmth and sexuality.

Sexual behaviour thereby becomes a symbol for social, political behaviour. Only through Love can the whole and the individual become true to itself.

Thus it is that Truth and Beauty are the proper concerns of artistic creation. But the mirror of theatre – if it shows us how things actually are – must include the portrayal of failure, inadequacy and fraud. So in reply to Ophelia's 'innocent' question whether Beauty could have a better companion than Honesty, Hamlet replies:

> *Ay, truly; for the power of Beauty will sooner transform*
> *Honesty from what it is to a bawd, than the force of*
> *Honesty can translate Beauty into his likeness.*

Honest aspiration, admiration, even love can so quickly become desire and lust – this is the way that Beauty undermines 'Honesty': this is the way that Claudius's love for Gertrude led to murder (and accompanied his desire to be King). "This...", Hamlet goes on to say...

> *..was sometime a paradox, but now the time gives it proof.*

The proof being in that act of Claudius.

So the Nature that "playing" holds the mirror up to is both the Reality which reveals the essence of Truth and Beauty, *and* the humdrum world where the inadequacy and deliberate wickedness of men present us with the failure to live in true relationship with Beauty.

The inadequacy of men is easily portrayed. Plays which limit their plots and metaphors to everyday human triviality – even including heartache and death treated with painful, earthly attention – are plentiful enough.

The question is: can theatre speak of that 'other' – can it hint at some 'Reality' which describes a world beyond our material, bodily 'reality'? Is this the realm of spirit? Does such reality exist?

That artists – even perhaps without knowing it – are in touch with such a world, would account for the compelling attraction that so much music and art exerts on us. Even such an apparently un-spiritual activity as ballroom dancing has its roots in elaborate ancient rituals which brought the dancers into communion with the spirit world. It may be that the frenzy of the discothèque is an attempt to recapture this: an attempt in a secular un-believing social vacuum to find some connection with a meaningful 'reality'.

At the time Shakespeare was writing, without doubt, everyone – or nearly everyone – believed in spirits, demons, God, the efficacy of religious faith, the unknown mysteries of a world beyond, behind, above, beneath our mortal existence. There may have been a number of atheists and doubters, but the real disputes (and dangers) concerned theological allegiance. While Islamic 'pagans' and Jews were outside the salvation of the Christian Church, Popish versus Protestant issues were the anguished dilemma of many in England: the switch from one to the other and back - and back again - being local village-church experience inside the 16th Century [5].

Shakespeare, cleverly and wisely, never allows that issue to intrude: and, though medieval demons inhabit the wood in *Midsummer Night's Dream*, and the Gods of Greek mythology feature in the stories he borrowed from Ovid, there is (surprisingly?) very little specific reference to the spirit world.

One of these rare moments occurs in the meeting of the twins - brother and sister - in *Twelfth Night*. Each believes that the other has been drowned in the shipwreck with which the play

---

[5] Henry VIII: 1536-39 Dissolution of the Monasteries, 1549 first English Prayer Book. 1553 Mary's return to Papal allegiance. 1558 Elizabeth re-establishes English Church.

begins. Viola, in order to survive in this strange country, disguises herself as a young man – basing her appearance exactly on her brother, Sebastian. So now he sees himself!

SEBASTIAN.   *Do I stand there? I never had a brother;*
Nor can there be that deity in my nature
Of here and everywhere. I had a sister
Whom the blind waves and surges have devour'd.
Of charity, what kin are you to me?
What countryman, what name, what parentage?

VIOLA.   *Of Messaline; Sebastian was my father.*
Such a Sebastian was my brother too;
So went he suited to his watery tomb;
If spirits can assume both form and suit,
You come to fright us.

SEBASTIAN.   *A spirit I am indeed,*
But am in that dimension grossly clad
Which from the womb I did participate.
Were you a woman, as the rest goes even,
I should my tears let fall upon your cheek,
And say 'Thrice welcome, drowned Viola!'

VIOLA.   *My father had a mole upon his brow.*

SEBASTIAN.   *And so had mine.*

VIOLA.   *And died that day when Viola from her birth*
Had numb'red thirteen years.

SEBASTIAN.   *O, that record is lively in my soul!*
He finished indeed his mortal act
That day that made my sister thirteen years.

VIOLA.   *If nothing lets to make us happy both*
But this my masculine usurp'd attire,
Do not embrace me till each circumstance
Of place, time, fortune, do cohere and jump
That I am Viola....

Twelfth Night V i 224 - 251

Sebastian's second and third lines mean: If I had God-like qualities I could be here and there at the same time – but those qualities I cannot have. Soon, however, he does claim that he has a spirit identity. This is in response to Viola's fear that he is a ghost – or rather a demon spirit that mimics her brother – "come to fright us".

But he is not a spirit in that sense. Rather he has (as everyone has) a soul existence which extends beyond this world, to which he has come (like everyone) by being born – via "the womb". And he has lived here...

...in that dimension grossly clad.

That is in a human body. This 'gross cladding' of flesh is the "muddy vesture" [vesture = clothing] mentioned in one of the (very few) other Shakespeare scenes in which the "immortal souls" possessed by all human beings are referred to. This is the scene at the end of *The Merchant of Venice* when Lorenzo instructs his stolen Jewish bride, Jessica, on the cosmology of angels and heavenly music that is witnessed by the stars:

> *Sit, Jessica. Look how the floor of heaven*
> *Is thick inlaid with patines of bright gold;*
> *There's not the smallest orb which thou behold'st*
> *But in his motion like an angel sings,*
> *Still quiring to the young-ey'd cherubins;*
> *Such harmony is in immortal souls,*
> *But whilst this muddy vesture of decay*
> *Doth grossly close it in, we cannot hear it.*

Merchant of Venice V i 58 - 65

The "immortal souls" – while they are still in the spirit realm – can hear the music: but we dressed in our "muddy" [= earthy/earthly] human bodies cannot.

So it is that in these two rare passages, Shakespeare invites us to acknowledge the spirit/soul reality, which, very likely, he believed in. But these are passing hints. There is no theology or preaching here – or anywhere in his writing. Rather it is that the poetry of the whole play offers us a constructed vision of a world of imagination which might be an echo of that spirit/soul reality.

This most beautiful conversation between Viola and her brother is a microcosm of Meaning: a tiny gem containing a picture of the relationship of Life to Eternity. Here, along with the question of soul identity are the little earthly recognitions of "a mole upon his brow" and the celebration of children's birthdays. Such things are the elements of our mortal life – and the coming together of the 'drowned', 'dead' twins an astounding metaphor for the fulfilment of life and hope.

During the play both Viola and Sebastian meet partners to whom they get married. The extraordinary beauty of the conversations between Viola (disguised as a boy) and her lover-to-be Orsino are echoed by the profound and bizarre conversations between Viola and Olivia – a lady who believes she is in love with a young man, and who then meets Sebastian, seizes him and marries him, because he *is* (or appears to be) that very man. The miracle that Sebastian experiences - meeting and falling in love with the most beautiful woman who instantly loves (and marries) him – parodies ultimate romance, but has him speak bewildering words on fantasy and wonder and reason [12ᵗʰ Night IV iii].

Though each of the twins love and marry, it is their re-union with each other that is the climax and poetic fulfilment of the play. Like marriage it is a union of male-female – but it presents an image of wholeness and togetherness which implies more than sexual union.

The world of Illyria is, as it were, the soul place. At the same time it is the material world: the place we find ourselves in. The two aristocratic households – of Count Orsino and the Lady Olivia – are organised by hierarchies of servants who give us an exact portrayal of the domestic arrangements of the aristocracy of Shakespeare's time. And the title of the play refers to the one day in the calendar when master-servant relationships are suspended and an anarchic reign of 'misrule' is allowed in the house. There is no such permitted suspension in the play but the atmosphere is close – and the Lady Olivia's fool, Feste, is described as an 'allowed fool' [I v 93]. Nevertheless these very English households are planted in Illyria which, though it may be geographically connected to the Adriatic coast, is an entirely mythical place suitable to host the fantastic adventures of Viola and Sebastian.

- - - - -

> **Aside.** This world is peopled with outrageous characters. As well as the memorable eccentricities of Belch and Aguecheek and Malvolio – surely three of the most intriguing roles that any actor could wish for – quietly in the background are the two sea Captains, mythical/symbolic messenger/servants who rescue the twins from the sea (itself a symbol of the unconscious). The first, un-named, assists Viola in her disguise and is linked into the end of the play when she remarks that he still has her "maiden weeds". The other, Antonio, has a strange adventurous backstory and is, at the end, silent and ignored. His passionate love for Sebastian is one more variation on the theme of heterosexual/homosexual love which throbs through the play.

- - - - -

At the same time, the main comic subplot – the gulling of Malvolio – extends the 'make-believe' of Theatre to its ultimate point.

When Malvolio finds and reads the forged letter which appears to tell him that Lady Olivia is in love with him, there is a conspiratorial collusion between the audience and the three people hidden on stage who watch and listen to him. When he turns and almost catches sight of them, we hold our breath in fear that he will see them – such is our identification with the watchers on stage. A little later Malvolio appears before Olivia in his yellow stockings (as the forged letter requested) and becomes so puffed up with proud illusion that he says to Sir Toby Belch "Go off, I discard you." Exit Malvolio. It is at this moment that a character called Fabian - who first appeared in the letter scene, rather as if a nondescript member of the audience had joined the conspirators on stage – makes the remark:

> *If this were played upon a stage now, I could condemn it as an improbable fiction.*
>
> **Twelfth Night III iv 129**

You mean it's *not* being "played upon a ......" ? Of course we know, but..... Bewilderment. Theatre, illusion, invention, imagination. Complicity and delight.

The joy of theatre.

And the extraordinary combination in this play, *Twelfth Night* [written very close to the time of *Hamlet* – but what a different sort of play!], of current social realism with the mythical adventures of Viola and Sebastian. It is another perfect Poetic Drama. And contains the line:

> *Prove true, imagination, oh prove true.*

..which might be another way of stating our hope of belief in what we see in the Mirror. In context it is spoken by Viola who has been accused by Antonio of betraying his friendship – he mistakes her for Sebastian and asks for his money. His passion demonstrates his sincerity; her confusion seeds the impossible possibility:

> *Methinks his words do from such passion fly*
> *That he believes himself; so do not I:*
> *Prove true imaginaton, oh prove true,*
> *That I, dear brother, be now ta'en for you.*
>
> **Twelfth Night III iv 382 - 385**

Passion, Imagination, Truth, Hope – the ingredients of a Shakespeare play. From the first debates about Substance and Shadow, through to the final miracle which is *The Tempest*, he holds us in thrall - even though it is "airy nothing".

It was back in 1596 that our master poet-playwright had Theseus complain:

> *The poet's eye, in a fine frenzy rolling,*
> *Doth glance from heaven to earth, from earth to heaven;*
> *And as imagination bodies forth*
> *The forms of things unknown, the poet's pen*
> *Turns them to shapes, and gives to airy nothing*
> *A local habitation and a name.*

Midsummer Night's Dream V i 12 - 17

Now, sixteen years later, as the play within the play vanishes, the magician Prospero reminds us:

> *Our revels now are ended. These our actors,*
> *As I foretold you, were all spirits, and*
> *Are melted into air, into thin air;*
> *And, like the baseless fabric of this vision,*
> *The cloud-capp'd towers, the gorgeous palaces,*
> *The solemn temples, the great globe itself,*
> *Yea, all which it inherit, shall dissolve,*
> *And, like this insubstantial pageant faded,*
> *Leave not a rack behind.*

The Tempest IV i 148 - 156

All 'insubstantial' stuff - only a shadow, only a dream, a reflection in a mirror, an allusive illusion.

But we, who have been in the theatre, have had a very real experience. Neither the cynical poet nor the material scientist can deny us that. After all, it is we who are...

> *Such stuff as dreams are made on.*

114

This is probably the order of writing of the plays, with generally agreed dates. Quotations appear on the pages numbered below.

ACKNOWLEDGEMENTS

My thanks to the many, many people who have taken part in The Shakespeare Workshop activities in the past twenty years in London, Oxford, Marcham, Stratford-on-Avon, Chichester, Edinburgh, Kiev, France and the Greek islands - for puzzling over Shakespeare's text, questioning and challenging interpretation. From a lifetime of theatre-going my debt of delight and inspiration is immeasurable: to the professional English stage, but equally to amateur and student groups - and the very special Shakespeare Reading Society where we read a play every month and recycle them all every three years. My thanks also to the many friends who have read parts of this book and offered comment: the remaining errors and peculiarities are entirely mine.

Tony Butler   June 2010